The
"I Hate Selling"
Book

The
"I Hate Selling"
Book

Business-building advice
for consultants, attorneys,
accountants,
engineers, architects, and
other professionals

Allan S. Boress

Library of Congress Cataloging-in-Publication Data

Boress, Allan S.
    The "I hate selling" book : business-building advice for consultants, attorneys, accountants, engineers, architects, and other professionals / Allan S. Boress.
        p. cm.
    Includes bibliographical references and index.
    ISBN 0-9709337-0-3
    1. Selling. 2. Consultants—Marketing. 3. Professions-
-Marketing. I. Title.
HF5438.25.B665 1994
658.85—dc20   94-33738
                                                    CIP

Printing number

10 9 8 7 6

Printed in the United States by
Morris Publishing • 3212 East Highway 30 • Kearney, NE 68847
1-800-650-7888

To
Dad
My hero.

Contents

Preface
How This Book Will Help You Become New- Business Driven

This is not a rehash of some sales book you've already read; rather, it was designed from scratch with you in mind. This book offers you a systematic approach to selling, one that has proved to be a real winner for people who sell *services* (rather than tangible items).

I wrote this book to help you and other professional service providers avoid the pain and suffering I experienced in the process of building my business. The skills and strategies presented will work for any professional service provider, including architects, accountants, doctors, attorneys, engineers, consultants, and those selling professional services for companies. Even those interested in changing jobs will benefit from this book. I created it to show you how to become a master of the art of selling professional services.

I wrote it for people who hate selling—as I do—but who have to do it anyway.

Specifically, in this book you'll discover how and where to:

- Sell more business by being a better qualifier, presenter, and closer
- Spot many more sales opportunities
- Outsell the competition in a competitive situation
- Boost your closing percentage to over 90 percent
- Get buyers to close themselves
- Find new business right now

- Overcome the pain of failure and rejection (finally!)
- Write custom-designed proposals that the buyer will want to see and buy immediately
- Get beyond selling on fees
- Create custom-designed presentations that will win the sale for you
- Find out, specifically, what the buyer's motives are without guesswork
- Get people to open up to you
- Determine if people are committed to action, and how to create that commitment
- Close the sale in a way that's painless for you and the buyer (and invisible to the buyer, too)
- Stay motivated
- Emulate the ways in which the top business producers in the professions have built their practices
- Use the telephone most effectively
- Determine if people can do business with you, or if you're wasting your time
- Build personal chemistry, and have people want to buy from you
- Discover and influence the decision-making process
- Listen in such a way that people will tell you exactly how to sell them

And much more, including showcase dialogues to help you witness how these techniques work in real selling situations.

Why Should You Read This Book?

That's for you to determine for yourself. After fourteen years of training thousands of consultants and people from all of the other professions, I've found that the ability to persuade someone to buy is the greatest skill in the world. In the end, it determines who will make it to the top of his or her profession.

After reading this book, you'll know more about selling professional services than 99 percent of your competition. I promise.

What are *your* career goals? This book will help you reach them.

Rainmakers and Divining Rods: Selling What You Don't See

New business is the lifeblood of every professional service firm. Some firms are going out of business, being forced into mergers or bought out, or slowly disintegrating before the owners' eyes because not enough new clients and new work are coming in.

Today, as the founders and rainmakers of numerous firms retire (or hope to), many see that their partners and staff simply aren't interested in or capable of growing the business.

Most firms were started and grown by entrepreneurs. Work was sold because it had to be in order for the founder to eat. Often, these entrepreneurs did such a good job of bringing in work that they had to hire others to help them with the workload. Customarily, those hired were not entrepreneurial by nature, but technical—they became service providers because they liked the kind of work the professions offered, not because they wanted to sell business.

The purpose of this book is to help you avoid some of the pain and suffering I and others have had to endure in the process of learning how to sell professional services effectively. My goal is to assist you in becoming much more comfortable with and successful at what I consider the Greatest Skill in the World. I hope to give you a much different perspective on what selling services really is.

My Promise

If you diligently follow the suggestions in this book, your sales success ratio, based on the experience of others who have done so, will improve to over 90 percent. Your pain of failure and fear of rejection will be permanently removed. And you will produce a great deal of new business in a very short period of time.

Why? Because there is no theory in this book. Over the past fourteen years as a sales, marketing, and client-retention consultant, I've had the good fortune to work with and get to know some of the best business developers (rainmakers) in the professions. In this book, you'll learn, systematically, what they and other highly successful business generators do to sell much more business than their competitors.

First, Some Background Information

I hate selling—with a passion! However, I do like it when people buy my services. Have you ever worked in a retail store? I have. There is a definite difference in the way retail businesses sell their products as opposed to the way professional service firms sell their services. Besides having the customer come to them, the retail salesperson has something tangible to show the customers. They can see it, feel it, smell it, touch it! They can identify the superiority of a product. Service providers who are selling and marketing are at a distinct disadvantage because they are not able to effectively show or present their intangible services.

After college, I worked in outside sales, which was quite different than retail. In outside sales, I had to find customers who didn't necessarily want to see me. Worse, people tried to manipulate me, lie to me, didn't show up for appointments, cancelled orders, and had bad credit. Face it, people treat salespeople differently than they treat other human beings! I felt used and abused.

Salespeople face a life of emotional ups and downs: the thrill of the sale, the agony of rejection and failure. It's this emotional roller coaster that causes approximately eight out of nine people who enter the field of sales to leave it. I did, too.

After a couple of years of misery, I went back to school at night. In 1976, I passed the CPA exam. At that point, I wanted to get as far away from customers and selling as I possibly could.

But was I shocked! From the very beginning of my career in public accounting, I found out that not only would I have to bring in business to attain the level of partnership, but I was selling every day! CPAs—and other service providers—whether they realize it or not, are always promoting their ideas to the client ("I think you should consider doing something about this excess inventory you have lying around."), to their bosses ("I need a raise."), to their co-workers ("Can I please get this typed?"), and to the IRS. Let's face it: who makes it to the top in any firm? Those who bring in business!

In 1980, I went into business for myself. It dawned on me that selling was a skill, just like public accounting and tax consulting. And, since I had become quite good at these skills, I felt that the skill of selling also could be learned and made easier. I bought every book and tape I could find on the subject. I took all of the courses, read all of the magazines. I was determined to learn how to sell.

The Greatest Skill

In November of 1980, I realized that selling is the "Greatest Skill in the World." You may recall that that was when we elected one of the greatest salespeople of this century, Ronald Reagan, to the presidency. It's generally accepted that he was not elected based on any special technical expertise that he had demonstrated as governor of

California (which is a good selling lesson for all service providers), but because we liked him better than the other guy.

Mr. Reagan, you'll remember, left office with one of the highest satisfaction ratings of all time. He was such a good salesman that George Bush was elected president on something called "repeat business." That's right: 80 percent of the voters interviewed in the exit polls who had voted for Reagan in 1980 voted for Bush. Your clients would kill for that kind of repeat business!

Using the Wrong System

Little that I read about selling worked for me. I wasn't positive, enthusiastic, or eloquent in the way I spoke or in my presentations. I had never been popular in school. My idea of a good time is being left alone to think and read—I don't really care to talk. I didn't consider myself a "people person." I was an accountant and a consultant. Because of those traits, I needed to create a methodology that I could feel comfortable with, and still get the job done.

I realized that every "professional" selling system I came across was initially developed to help salespeople sell tangible products, like office copiers, to purchasing agents and office managers. What I'd seen and heard had basically been schmoozed up, given technical language, and made more complicated. It seemed like those teaching "professional selling" had basically exchanged the word *salesperson* for the word *professional*.

I was selling an intangible product, consulting services, to business owners, CEOs, and managing partners of professional firms. Using the incorrect selling system was as wrong as hiring a corporate attorney to defend you for murder in a jury trial.

In selling services, you must realize that people buy other people, not professional firms. There is no copy machine or computer for clients to see or touch. No matter what firm you work for, prospective customers buy because of the individuals who will be interacting with them—they have no other source of reference.

Firms that are much more qualified to do the work, big-name firms, often lose to less competent or less well known competitors because clients wouldn't know a good audit, piece of software, or legal brief if it hit them in the face. Clients can only gauge results, and the way the service is delivered. And the results can't be evaluated until after the professional is hired.

Therefore, instead of sales training per se, I began to study those masters of the art of selling services: physicians. Doctors don't sell, you say? Boy, have they got you fooled! Even though they don't look like salespeople, act like them, or put on flashy presentations, doctors are selling all of the time. In addition to all of the unnecessary surgery that is performed in this country, doctors are constantly selling their patients on their treatments.

I studied medical journals, interviewed physicians, and read articles on the way doctors conduct patient interviews. Today, selling is very different for me. Rather than me hustling to sell my services, my prospective clients do much of the work, in a process that is quite comfortable for everyone.

The Good News

In this book, you'll learn how to conduct a *sales examination*, a systematic approach that is often much the opposite of the outdated and old-fashioned sales techniques created for selling products. It's designed to have the prospective client do more of the work, be time effective, and be adjustable to your own style. It will also put you in total control of the sales process.

It is my belief that we service providers have the best possible tools to be highly effective bringing in business (skills that only the very best salespeople have). All we need to do is enhance and shift those skills to a business-development mode (see Exhibit 1).

A Special Request

This is not a conventional sales book. Many of the ideas may be new to you. My goal is not to turn you into a salesperson but to help you become highly effective at closing more sales systematically and painlessly. Therefore, I request you to approach the contents of this book with an open mind.

Professionals are highly intelligent people. We also tend to be quite suspicious and critical. We're good investigators and are generally always looking for what's wrong. That's the nature of our work: Find out what's wrong and fix it. In this book, look for what's right, instead.

Since this book was written for all people who sell intangible services, the various sample conversations included are drawn from a number of different professions. At first glance, you may think that there aren't enough examples for your particular situation. Please!

Exhibit 1. Shifting your professional skills to a business-development mode.

USE YOUR ALREADY EXISTING ADVANTAGES
to Succeed at Business Development

CONSULTANTS	TOP BUSINESS PRODUCERS
• Expert diagnosticians	
• Inquisitive and curious by nature	
• Intelligent	
• Persistent and Consistent	
• Accustomed to asking questions	
• Nonthreatening	
• Trustworthy	
• Organized/systematic	
• Perceived as business experts	
• Already have powerful contacts in community	
• Project oriented	
• Should know their clients' hurts, ability to pay, and decision-making process	

Look for the similarities, not the differences. I've trained every possible kind of consultant, attorney, engineer, accountant, interior designer, job hunter, and so on. What you will learn here works! Of course, there are always unique quirks in each profession, but I've found that this selling system applies to all.

Be aware that I have helped thousands of professional service providers become much more successful at selling over the last fourteen years. Let me coach you, too. Using the tools and techniques in this book, you have a *divining rod,* a point of departure leading to *new business.*

A Preview

To give you an idea of how the selling plan in this book works and to motivate you, I have included a copy of a communication I recently received from a client. The client is a managing partner of a CPA firm and the memo in Exhibit 2 is one he circulated to his fellow partners. It describes how the selling plan detailed in this book worked successfully in an actual situation.

Study, enjoy, and sell more business!

Exhibit 2. How these techniques helped a professional sell more business.

MEMO

TO: Mike, Jerry, Randy, Gwen, Jim, Kris, Pete, Joan, Allan

FROM: MFS

RE: The Sales Technique

The following is an example of how we recently sold a client our services. Had Pete and I not used Allan's techniques, we probably wouldn't have gotten this engagement.

This company received our name from an existing client and called us. Based on a couple of questions that I asked, the caller talked for about ten minutes concerning his business. His comments were then used to prepare expanded questions for our initial meeting.

In our initial meeting, we did very little talking and a lot of listening. The client probably talked for 80 to 90 percent of the time. He told us the following:

1. He was not getting any tax planning from his current accountant.
2. His general ledger was not being properly utilized.
3. His in-house bookkeeper had accounting and computer deficiencies.
4. He was not getting timely service.

Before we left, I indicated that we could begin work immediately. However, he wanted to know more about our fee structure and wanted to receive a proposal. We walked out of there with a firm commitment to speak in two days in order to set up our next meeting.

For the second meeting, we took the pains that were expressed in the first meeting and designed a four-step proposal to meet the company's needs. When we set up the meeting, however, we were not able to be the last people in. Had we known the importance of being the last ones in, we would have tried a different approach in setting up the meeting. During this meeting, we asked if there were any additional questions and then did a quick review of our proposal. We again attempted to close the deal at that session, but he indicated that he was not going to make a decision for another three or four days.

The new client called us in four days and said that we were selected. He also indicated that he wanted to let me know why we were selected. His comments were as follows:

1. We were not the most moderately priced firm that he had talked to; however . . .
2. We listened.
3. We were the only ones to address his needs.

In summary, we took the things that we learned at the first meeting, since they were obviously his pains, and structured our proposal accordingly. In my mind, there is no doubt that we let this new client sell himself. Had we used our traditional techniques, we probably would not have gotten this company as a client since we would have been perceived as no different than anybody else and since our fees were not the lowest.

:skr

Acknowledgments

I have been fortunate to have been mentored in selling by many generous and loving people over the years. They deserve to be recognized and thanked: Barry Boress, Sandy Rubens (of beloved memory), Jordon Rubens, Terry Slattery, Mike Cummings, Steve Taback, and Brian Azar. Thank you.

Some of the contents of this book have been excerpted from my "I-Hate-Selling" course which is produced by the American Institute of Certified Public Accountants. All excerpts are reprinted with their permission.

Special thanks to my wonderful and supportive wife, Christine; and to Stella Ashen, my Director of Marketing, who edited the book, for her excellent contributions throughout.

Part One

Professionals And Selling

1

Why Service Providers Don't Sell More Business

Most service providers close about 20 percent of the business opportunities they get, but they really could be closing 90 percent or more. These service providers are losing this new business due to their ignorance, inertia, and inaction.

Most professionals don't understand selling, although they may think they do. In order for you to become more effective at selling professional services, let's take a look at what holds professional service providers back from selling more work. These explanations reflect input from discussions with thousands of consultants, attorneys, engineers, architects, designers, accountants, and other professionals over the last fourteen years.

"I Have No Time to Sell"

Chances are that answer spilled right out of your mouth! After all, who's got time to sell? We're supposed to be billable—that's how many of us are compensated. When I first got started in public accounting, my boss wanted me to be charged out 110 percent of the time.

Indeed, lack of spare time in one's work day is the foremost justification for not bringing in more work. And it is a valid reason. After all, professionals aren't salespeople. Salespeople are supposed to be spending all of their time selling and servicing their customers. We have work that must get finished.

Of course, the lack of time does give those not inclined to sell a handy excuse. In fact, there are very busy professionals who do find the time to sell, even during their busiest time of the year, because they really want to.

There is a part of every work day that is an absolutely perfect time to sell more business: lunchtime! For important psychological reasons that I'll get into later, lunch is one part of every day that is usually spent alone or with one's partners or staff. Even during our busiest days, we usually find time to eat. Why not invest some of those lunchtimes with clients, referral sources, prospective clients? Not every day, perhaps. Consider utilizing four-to-twelve lunches (or breakfasts or dinners) a month to sell more business. Chances are it'll be four-to-twelve times more than the great majority of your competition.

"Personal Marketing Skills Aren't Required For Partnership or Advancement in My Firm"

Even in today's competitive environment, there are still some firms that promote staff who don't have the slightest disposition to bring in business. In those cases, what the firm often winds up with are staff members earning partnership salaries without bearing the burden of contributing new lifeblood to the firm.

Be careful about the message you are sending to your staff. Are they abundantly aware that in order to attain partnership or ownership they will have to prove that they can bring in business? Don't wait for them to be motivated to do so once they are made partners. By then it could be too late.

"I Don't Like Selling"

No fooling? Maybe that's one reason you became a consultant, engineer, or dentist. If you loved selling, chances are you would have pursued a career in sales.

I hate selling. In this book you'll find a different way to sell, one that won't turn you into a "salesperson" and has been custom-designed for professional service providers.

"I Don't Know How to Sell Myself Effectively"

We professionals tend to be quite risk-averse by nature and only embark on those pursuits we feel confident about. My goal is to give you the skills to be much more confident about your ability to sell more effectively, immediately upon finishing this book.

"There is No Novocaine for the Pain of Failure"

Are you fond of failure? As professionals we're not allowed to fail—or we could wind up getting sued.

Unfortunately, the message of "No failure allowed" usually permeates the firm at every level, for every function, including bringing in business. Professionals won't take risks where there is a likely possibility they will be condemned for failure.

In selling professional services, one must fail to succeed. The more you fail, the more business you will sell. So, failure to bring in business must be allowed, and even actively promoted, to give professionals the freedom to succeed at selling.

"I Assume My Clients Know What They Need and Will Ask for It When They're Ready"

Many of us are reluctant to approach our clients about what we feel they need for fear of damaging the relationship. This fear is not without basis; people, in general, do not like being "sold."

However, by not approaching clients for additional work, we leave them wide-open to interlopers—outsiders who sometimes wind up getting the kind of work we could do just as well. For instance, your client may consult with an outsider as to what computer system to buy, yet who knows the client's records and systems better than you?

By not being forthcoming with our clients when we should be, we are opening the door also to outsiders who have their own coterie of professionals they like working with. They can, and often will, introduce competitors to our clients.

In addition, when we're not proactive about suggesting other services, our clients' businesses may not be as healthy and successful as they should be. Maybe our clients would be less concerned about fees if they made more money, too. We must be proactive to be successful. Don't *assume* your clients know what they need; *presume* that they need what you think they do, and work from there.

"I Have No Set Action Plan"

Professionals like to create lists; we need systems and action plans. Without a list of activities to follow, we generally stall and do little or nothing.

Imagine trying to accomplish a consulting engagement, a jury trial, or any type of professional service without a plan of action; the job probably wouldn't run smoothly or be as successful as it could be. The same holds true for accomplishing a personal sales plan.

Set goals for the number of face-to-face contacts you will have every week with clients, prospective clients, and referral sources. Start with three a week. At the end of a year, you will have had over 150 opportunities you might not otherwise have had.

"I'm Not Held Accountable"

In one regard, we professionals are like children. Unless we're held accountable by our firms, little business will be developed except by those who are good at it and therefore enjoy it.

Those firms that have the highest participation by the partnership and staff in bringing in business are either blessed with a collection of people who are good at selling or their people actively hold each other accountable for bringing in work. Some firms tie compensation directly to the amount of new business brought in.

"There Is No Support or Recognition from the Firm"

Most service providers aren't motivated to change their behavior by money unless it represents a very material part of the total compensation package. Firms have tried, and often failed, to motivate (usually staff) through bonuses or awards.

Fortunately, the professions generally afford us a comfortable means of support. One important way to motivate staff and partners is psychologically. Make business developers the heroes of the firm. Shower attention and admiration on them. Publicize their efforts generously.

"There Are No Firm-Wide Goals"

If your firm doesn't have a set goal for growth or new business brought in, any expansion will be by accident. People like to participate in team efforts where everyone is on the same wavelength. They need to know what is expected and wanted of them.

One of my clients, a regional engineering firm, had stagnated for years, but the principals couldn't figure out why. We discovered the problem was that everyone was doing their own thing—the principals had never taken the time to organize the firm's business development efforts or to set goals for the next few years.

Once that was done, the goals were broken down per principal (partner), and each had a personal marketing plan-of-action to help reach the goals. The firm goals for each year were publicized to everyone in the firm and constantly reinforced through all of the in-house newsletters and at principal and staff meetings. In addition, each person carried his own goal written on a piece of paper in his wallet so he could refer to it constantly.

After only nine months, the firm had reached its first-year goal of a 16 percent increase in business over the previous year. This happened because everyone was on the same path: a shared goal that was constantly emphasized to the entire staff created the momentum, drive, and strategies necessary to increase business.

"The Firm Leaders Do Not Participate"

Sometimes, firms bring me in to work only with their staff to bring in more business. The partners aren't interested; they consider business-development to be beneath them.

Forget it! That approach doesn't work; partners must lead the way. Staff will follow the lead of the managing partner and partnership as to bringing in business. If the partners do it and it is well-publicized (and expected), others will as well. If the partners don't, nothing much will happen.

Diagnosis and Rx: Schedule a Daily Business Development Workout

In this chapter we have looked at eleven reasons why professionals don't sell more work:

1. They have no time to sell.
2. Personal marketing skills aren't required for partnership or advancement.
3. They don't like selling.
4. They don't know how to sell themselves effectively.
5. The firm doesn't provide any "novocaine" for those who fail.

6. They presume clients know what they need and will ask for it when they're ready.
7. The firm has no set action plan.
8. They are not held accountable.
9. There is no support or recognition by the firm.
10. There are no firm-wide goals.
11. The firm leaders do not participate.

Perhaps I've missed some. The point is that these are not acceptable reasons for failing to sell more business. These are simply "excuses" that may be holding you (and others in your firm) back. You must forget these, if you want to succeed.

Your Sales Prescription: The "I Hate Selling" Action Plan

- Even with your busy schedule, you must create the time to sell new business by meeting clients, prospective clients, and referral sources for breakfast, lunch, or dinner. Set appointments today for the next four weeks. Do not be afraid to set these kinds of appointments for far in the future—your most precious asset is time and you need to plan these meetings.
- Technical skills are not enough anymore; to succeed in the long run, you have to bring in new business. Become committed, starting today, to being as proficient at selling as you are in your technical and professional skills.
- You don't have to like selling, you just have to do it. So, stop complaining and start doing! Your selling skills will improve dramatically with the tactics learned in this book.
- Believe it or not, as a professional, you already have the skills you need to be a great salesperson; you merely need to apply these skills to business development.
- In trying to sell more business, you will fail; nobody sells everybody. The sooner you accept this, the easier it becomes to brush off rejection and move on to the next prospect.
- Don't assume your clients know what services they need and will ask for them accordingly; rather, presume that you know what they need and make sure to discuss your recommendations with your clients.
- Just as you would create a plan for completing a job, use the same concept to create a systematic action plan to bring in business. Make a list right now of people you should be talking to: prospective clients, existing clients, and referral sources.

- Make sure your associates and your firm hold people accountable for bringing in more business. People who generate business should be well compensated and lauded as heroes in the office.
- Set firm-wide and individual goals. Publicize these goals to all staff members and emphasize what each individual must do to achieve these goals.
- Partners and principals must lead the way in emphasizing and carrying out business-development efforts, because staff will only follow these leaders. If the partners aren't involved in bringing in more business, nothing much will happen.

2

The Eight Universal Traits of the Top Business Producers In The Professions

When you want to learn a new skill, how do you go about it? Do you strive to "recreate the wheel" or solicit the advice of the average Joe? Or would you want to learn from someone who is already eminently successful in that area?

Happily, I realized early in my quest to master everything important about the skill of selling professional services that I could learn a lot from the people who were already doing it well. As I got to know these powerful rainmakers, I found that they are alike in many ways.

Common Character Traits

The numerous rainmakers I've interviewed and worked with over the years are quite similar to each other in several aspects of their personalities, although they're certainly not clones or typical salespeople. Let's examine what personality traits these people have in common and see if those top business producers you know share these attributes. Here are the eight common traits I've discovered in the best business developers in all of the professions.

1. *They know that new business is the lifeblood of the firm.* There are quite a few gurus to the professions who travel the country telling people how to run more profitable practices. Often, the core of their advice is to make the busines smaller by cutting staff and the "less

desirable" clients. That makes a lot of sense, marketing-wise, doesn't it? Isn't that what the folks in Detroit did in the 1970s and 1980s, especially when the Japanese targeted the compact car market and the value of the dollar plummeted in relation to the yen? Didn't Detroit decide to make fewer, but more profitable, cars? And didn't the car makers fall on some terribly difficult times doing that?

You see, it seems logical to consolidate your practice and eliminate all but the cream of the crop. But when you do, you are also cutting your market share, your word-of-mouth advertising, and your influence in the marketplace. If you are looking to do less business, then consolidation is a good choice for you, because you can manage yourself right out of business by consolidating.

Professionals are notorious for concentrating on profit margins and the bottom line, while ignoring the top line or gross revenues. That can be great news for you—if you decide not to consolidate, but rather to build up your own book of business. If much of your competition is looking to cut back, you've got a wide-open marketplace for yourself and a handful of others.

The top business producers in the professions know that nothing stays the same. You're either moving forward or moving back. To cut back on business is like infecting the body mechanism with cancer—it negatively affects the attitude of everyone in the firm and the health of the business. This generally results in the eventual death of the entity.

New business provides enthusiasm and new learning. It creates new opportunities, allowing you to keep the best people over the long term so that they don't leave and become your competitors. Sure, it's harder to manage a growing practice than a shrinking one, and you're not going to want every piece of new business that comes in the front door. But whoever said success was easy?

2. *They are positive and optimistic with existing and prospective clients and with referral sources.* This attribute is generally the opposite of many good professional service providers; they tend to be critical, negative, and skeptical—characteristics that help make them good at their jobs but can hurt them in client relationships. The rainmakers in the professions have learned that they need to be positive around their clients, but critical about the issues facing their clients' businesses.

Prospective clients are much more attracted to positive people, because positive feelings rub off on those around them. These feelings tend to give the clients a sense of hope, which they will greatly appreciate!

Since the very nature of the professions involves looking for what's wrong and then fixing it, negatives are considered good and positives are looked upon with caution. Consider the computer consultant who discovers the hidden glitch in her client's invaluable computer operations—by bringing it to her client's attention, she will be rewarded for a job well done. Consider the accountant who discovers employee theft at his client's premises—again, the client would see value in this discovery. However, clients see little value in the pessimistic service-provider when there's nothing wrong.

At least 90 percent of all professionals I've met are critical and negative by nature. But this type of personality does not attract prospective clients or keep existing clients happy most of the time. It's a fact: People are attracted to positive people, and the true business developer understands there's a time to be positive in his or her business.

Jill is a top producing partner at a national law firm. Although she was handed a large amount of business when a partner retired three years ago, she has since tripled it. She explains how she was able to do this: "My clients and future clients have enough problems in their lives as it is. I go *out of my way* to look for what's good about their business and personal situations, and tell them about that too. This boosts their self-esteem and makes them feel better about themselves and about me as their service provider. My competitors don't even think of looking for anything beyond what's wrong. I attract business because I give my clients and referral sources the psychological support and reinforcement they often don't get at home or at work."

The good news is that this quality of the top business producers is one you can easily acquire. No additional coursework or study is necessary—you merely have to decide that you want to be positive and optimistic around your existing and prospective clients. As a CPA and consultant, I used to think it was my job to tell my clients constantly where they were messing up. Now, I make a conscious effort to take a much more positive approach in dealing with them.

3. *People feel comfortable around them.* Although they may strike terror in the hearts of those who work for them, rainmakers—no matter how tremendously successful they are—have the ability to make people they meet feel at ease in their presence.

In the beginning, I thought that it would be very difficult to work for and consult with the managing partners of professional service firms—they're so successful! But just the opposite occurred: These powerful individuals have been among the nicest people I've met. They make me feel at home and treat me like royalty. It's very likely that this skill of creating a comfortable atmosphere is one reason they rose to the top.

People generally only hire and do business with people they like and are comfortable with. Also, from a selling standpoint, it is this vital skill of putting people at ease which prepares and allows prospective clients to open up and tell the service-provider what the real issues are—how they can, in fact, be sold.

The good news is that this is a skill you can develop; it will be covered in Chapter 6.

4. *They laugh at themselves.* One of my mentors told me that selling was merely hysterical activity on the way to the grave. Rainmakers tend to put the proper perspective on selling. It's not the end of the world if they don't get the next client or sell the next project; they don't lose a lot of sleep over it. Sure, you say, it would be easy to adopt this attitude if one was already successful. Nonetheless, they adopted this attitude early on in their selling careers. It gives them the freedom to press forward without ruminating on their defeats (which are many if one is actively selling).

The good news is that you can make the decision to adopt this attitude of the best business developers. You can learn to laugh at your setbacks more often, if you want to.

5. *They are very good listeners.* Ever notice that you didn't learn very many success-oriented skills in school? Did you learn how to set goals and accomplish them? Did you learn how to maintain and improve personal and business relationships? How to run a small business? Did instructors even teach you how to study? Probably not. Unfortunately, we were left to our own devices to learn (or miss) many of the skills necessary to be productive in the real world.

School didn't teach us how to be effective listeners, either. Listening is one way rainmakers separate themselves from their competition; they give clients and prospective clients the freedom and space to talk frequently, and about anything. It is this behavior, which one usually could expect only from one's best friend or a loved one, that attracts other people to do business with them. Always remember in selling professional services, people buy other people.

The good news is that this is a skill you can improve, and it will be covered in Chapter 6.

6. *They're givers, not takers.* The best business producers tend to be team-builders. They care deeply about their clients and are con-

cerned with how they can best serve them. They're not the back-stab-bers one might expect from someone who brings in a lot of business. They look out for the interests of those who work for them and for their referral sources. They aim to give and keep on giving and then, perhaps, to receive.

When I frequent "networking events," it seems everyone is out to get something for themselves. That's not the behavior of many of the rainmakers that I've met in situations like that: They attend in order to give, not to receive. They use social opportunities to direct business to their clients, to play matchmaker for a referral source, or simply to help someone. They believe that what they give away they will receive back tenfold. It is this giving attitude that attracts people to them, including prospective clients.

7. *They are righteous believers in their ability to perform and the value of their services.* There's no other way to put it—the top business pro-ducers I've met are totally convinced of their ability (and that of their staff) to do the absolutely best job for the prospective client. They be-lieve that people who don't select their firm to do the work are crazy!

It's this attitude that also often removes fee objections and com-promises, because top producers believe they are worth every cent that they are paid (and then some). Always remember that you are paid in direct proportion to what you believe you are worth.

Much of our communication is nonverbal. Often, it's not what we say that comes across most strongly; rather, the prospective client will most likely pick up on what we feel and unconsciously project.

Rainmakers sell more than their competition because they are more confident about the services they and their firms perform. If the seller is unsure, the buyer will easily pick up on this, causing the sale to be lost as the buyer becomes afraid of a failed project. If the rain-maker is not confident about his or her ability to perform a particular service, he or she will bring along an expert to the meeting who is.

The first sale you have to make is to yourself. You have to believe and be sold first. You have to be 100 percent convinced that, if you were in the buyer's shoes, you would buy the proposed service at the offered fee. The good news is that you can become more confident about and more successful with what you have to sell. I'll discuss how later in the Rx section of this chapter.

8. *They enjoy what they do and the people they work with.* The best business developers love what they do and wouldn't change it for the world. Of course, some might prefer to work fewer hours—because they tend to have a larger client load than those who don't bring in

much work. But, overall, they are happy in their vocation and with their co-workers.

It's almost impossible to sell work that you don't want to do or will have to perform with people you don't like. The good news is that this characteristic of the best business developers is under your control as well. You have the power to take a new and fresh look at your work and decide to like it and appreciate it more.

Diagnosis and Rx: Become a Fit Business Developer

In this chapter I have discussed the universal traits of the top business producers in the professions. Remember: the more you emulate the characteristics of these rainmakers, the more likely you are to share their success.

Review these traits and try to adopt and adapt them in your professional life:

- ▸ *They know that new business is the lifeblood of the firm.* As I stated in Chapter 1, there are no acceptable excuses for not selling business. In these competitive times, you will never reach a high level in your profession unless you are able to bring in new work. So, accept the fact that selling is a necessity, and apply yourself to getting the job done.
- ▸ *They are positive and optimistic with existing and prospective clients and with referral sources.* Use your critical skills for unearthing client problems, but make an effort to be positive and optimistic in your client relationships. Clients are people too— they don't want to hear only the bad news. Here's a practice pointer for you: When meeting with clients to update them on their situations, make yourself use a "good news, bad news" format—along with the bad news, give them the good news (find some!). The more you look for the silver lining, the easier it will be. Someday, you may even find yourself giving good news *without* bad news—that's okay! Your clients will appreciate your positive attitude, and it will lead to more business.
- ▸ *People feel comfortable around them.* Although they are successful and powerful, rainmakers have a way of putting people at ease. They are gracious and see others as human beings, not just as numbers or machinery. They make others feel important—without licking their boots.

  Try to think of situations where you felt comfortable; what

sort of treatment put you at ease! Was it the environment? The attitude? Probably some of each. Do your best to treat people well and to make them comfortable with you.

▸ *They laugh at themselves.* Top producers are very dedicated and earnest about the quality of the work they do, but they don't take themselves too seriously. Every time I talk with successful service providers about their office environment, they invariably say something like, "It's a great place to work. Everybody works hard but has fun. We give a lot but get a lot in return." This attitude is very conducive to bringing in business. So, remember to lighten up and laugh at yourself once in a while; have some fun. That demeanor will serve you well with internal and external customers.

▸ *They are very good listeners.* The best business producers listen much more than they talk. They know that by being quiet they'll learn more about other individuals and their needs. Also, clients and others greatly appreciate being listened to, which helps establish a good relationship and leads to more business. If you do more than 20 percent of the talking in a selling situation, you're doing something wrong. You must do whatever it takes to keep yourself from dominating the conversation. Instead of blabbering away, ask relevant questions, and then sit back and take notes while the client gives you the information you need to make the sale.

▸ *They're givers, not takers.* You might think that the most successful business producers are focused on "What's in it for me?" Actually, the opposite is true. These rainmakers tend to be deeply concerned about the best interests of their clients, referral sources, co-workers, and people in general. For example, when they attend a networking function, they tend to focus on finding business for their clients. This attitude brings them great rewards in the long run.

Try to focus on how you can enrich the lives of others. What can you do to make life better for your clients, co-workers, and so on? If you adopt this giving attitude, prospective clients and others will naturally be drawn to you, and your practice will thrive.

▸ *They are righteous believers in their ability to perform and the value of their services.* Rainmakers are supremely secure in the knowledge that they can get the job done well, and this attitude comes across as they relate to others. Most communication is nonverbal, so it's not necessarily what they say that expresses this confidence and ability. That's why it's so important that the first sale you make be to yourself: you must be 100 percent convinced that if you were in the buyer's shoes, you would buy the proposed services at the offered fee. If you have sold yourself, your certainly and self-assurance will intrinsically help you sell others too.

Here's an exercise I've used successfully with thousands of professionals just like you. Stop what you are doing and write down twenty-five reasons why people must do business with you. Forget reasons like "good service." Everybody says that. Instead, be specific by considering the successes you've helped provide your clients or employers in the past.

Use the REVRB (pronounced reverb) method to fully discern your value and to have your clients see it too. Write down your twenty-five reasons with respect to:

- Relationships: The nature of the relationships you have with your clients
- Experience: Your experience in their industry with businesses or situations like theirs
- Value: The value you provide
- Results: The results you helped them produce in their businesses
- Business: The ways you've helped their businesses grow

This exercise will sell you on the value of your services, and it's the foundation for sales presentations that sell. (I'll discuss presentations in depth in Chapters 10, 11, and 12.)

▸ *They enjoy what they do and the people they work with.* The best business developers love what they do and wouldn't change it for the world. It's almost impossible to sell work that you don't want to do or will have to perform with people you don't like. So, take a fresh look at your work and office environment and decide to like it and appreciate in more. Change whatever you need to in order to make this possible.

3

Selling Ain't Marketing—But You Need Both to Survive In the 21st Century

Last year, I conducted some full-day programs for a professional association on the campus of a local college. Wandering into the campus bookstore, I found a handsome marketing text filled with four-color glossies; it was approximately 400 pages long. Since the copyright was the current year, I presume it was state-of-the-art—it certainly looked it. Guess how many of the 400 pages were devoted to the marketing of professional services. 200? 150? No—just *one*. That's right, one whole page was dedicated to marketing professional services. And the authors' idea of professional service firms was credit card companies and airlines.

A Little Background

The art of marketing and selling professional services is a relatively new one. Although professionals have always had to market their services because of the transactional nature of their business, it is only in the last fifteen years or so that the professions have been allowed to actively promote their services via the media and through active solicitation of prospective clients. Procuring clients is now an open field, limited only by one's imagination, time constraints, drive, and budget.

A lot of mistakes have been made in marketing professional services. Many firms still market and sell their services as if they were tangible goods, like computers. Unfortunately, it's not that easy. In selling and marketing services, there is nothing to see, feel, taste, or smell.

All we have to market and sell as professionals is ourselves! No matter what firm you work for, people buy other people; they buy the individuals they interact with. This explains why we sometimes lose business to less-qualified firms. It also explains why you don't have people ordering your services over the phone with their credit cards. Do you get a lot of walk-in traffic?

It's important to create a distinction between marketing services and selling services because they are very different in purpose. We don't want to expect results from marketing that can only be accomplished through active selling.

Marketing Defined

Here's my definition of marketing professional services:

Marketing is *anything* that puts you in front of someone you want to do business with.

This perception frees you to be creative; it recognizes that any contact you have with clients, prospective clients, and referral sources is marketing. The only marketing I have ever found that works on a consistent basis is personal marketing. All the fancy brochures, ad campaigns, and even TV commercials that you see can only act as an adjunct and a support to effective personal marketing—not as a replacement. And good marketing can only provide the opportunity; people still have to be sold by a human being.

Many service providers have become disenchanted with marketing because they expected business to increase substantially if they simply hired a marketing director, advertised, distributed handsome brochures, and/or sent direct mail. These techniques work for products, like soup or television sets, but they aren't effective for services. Sadly, all marketing can be expected to do is provide the *opportunity*. If marketing guaranteed sales, you wouldn't need to read this book! All you would have to do is set aside a certain percent of gross revenues for advertising, and you could expect a good return on investment.

I've seen professional service firms waste tens of thousands of dollars (in one instance, over a million) on seminars and other market-ing efforts with no results at all. That's why selling is so important.

What Selling Is Not

Here's what selling is not: Selling is not convincing someone to do something. Have you ever tried to convince someone to do some-thing? How effective is it? Are you married? Do you have children? I rest my case.

You see, in selling, as in physics, for every action there is an equal and opposite reaction. One of my mentors taught me that you cannot convince anyone to do anything; they have to discover it for them-selves. You cannot convince anyone to buy something, either. They have to see the value for themselves and want to buy for their own reasons.

Yes, you can drive people crazy over a period of time by pestering them, and they may eventually give up. But they will usually resent you for it and often will back out of their commitment. This is not a very time-efficient or effective approach!

Selling is not talking either. Some people think that the more you talk to someone, or at someone, the more likely they are to buy. Please absorb this early on: People couldn't care less about what you have to say! People care most about what they have to say. The prob-lem is that most people who sell don't give prospective clients the opportunity to talk because they think that selling is talking.

Selling Redefined

Here are four definitions of selling that I'd like to review with you. They are all different, but they work together nicely. I request that you put aside your already existing beliefs and opinions and maintain an open mind, because these definitions work:

1. *Technically, selling is what we do once we are in front of a prospective client.* Marketing gets us there; selling is our behavior once we're there.

2. *Selling is just a conversation.* That's right, selling is just a conver-sation, similar to many other conversations you have during the day. One of the reasons professionals are held back in their selling ability is their fear of the sales process. I've discovered that selling is akin to

many chats you have every day. However, instead of the title of this conversation being "Sports" or "Relationships," it's "The Possibility of Doing Business."

3. *Selling is a sorting process.* That's all selling is—it's a sort. In selling, all you want to do is sort the yes's from the no's as quickly, effectively, and painlessly as possible.

Your goal is to sort those people who will do business with you from those who will not. Some will fall in the yes pile, some will fall in the no pile. That's okay; nobody sells everybody. Even Ronald Reagan, "the Great Communicator," did not get everyone's vote, and relatively few people drive Chryslers despite the efforts of the best salesperson in that business, Lee Iacocca.

Marketing provides the opportunity to get in front of prospects, and selling is the manner in which you determine which of them will become your clients. In a sense, marketing is the strategy that will bring you the opportunity for more business, and selling is the tactic that—employed properly—will actually grow your practice.

4. *Selling is an examination.* In keeping with the analogy of the physician as the ideal role model for being effective at selling, I would like you to begin looking at selling as more of an examination of someone's ability to buy rather than anything else. In this book you will learn how to "examine" a prospective client.

It took me a long time to figure out, but I finally realized that all of the people who had done business with me over the years possessed certain qualifications. In each instance, there were certain determining factors that had to exist for me to make the sale.

In every selling situation you were ever in, in every sale you've ever made, the prospective client displayed certain characteristics and abilities that facilitated the sale.

I discovered that if these qualifications existed, or if I could facilitate their being—based upon my examination of the selling situation—the result of the sale had very little to do with my ability as seller, and my closing percentage of success was way over 95 percent (remember, nobody sells everybody). If there was an exception to my sales test, the sale couldn't be made.

This discovery made me feel quite good. It removed so many of the feelings of fear and rejection I had suffered in the past when people told me no. I knew that my job was now to effectively test the selling situation to determine whether prospective clients were qualified, whether they had the ability to do business with me. If I did a good job of testing the selling situation and they didn't buy, I could always trace the reason to an exception on my sales examination.

Don't be concerned if this is confusing; Part Two will guide you to the successful implementation of the sales examination tests.

Diagnosis and Rx: Understanding What Ails You Will Lead to a Cure

‣ The need to market and sell is relatively new for professionals. However, don't fool yourself into thinking that your skills will sell themselves; in this competitive marketplace, personal marketing and selling are absolutely necessary in order for you to survive and thrive in the twenty-first century. You must learn how to wisely invest your marketing budget (another necessity) and how to close more business. By reading this book, you're well on your way.

‣ Marketing is anything that puts you in front of someone you want to do business with. This includes such things as advertisements, sending relevant articles to clients, seminars, being involved in business and social groups, volunteer work, and so on. The most valuable marketing is personal marketing—anything that puts you in direct contact with a client, potential client, or referral source, because when purchasing professional services the customer or client is really buying you. The personal contact you have with important individuals greatly expedites and facilitates the buying process. That is, the more targeted people you meet (target individuals in the industries and income levels you are most comfortable working with), the more clients you are likely to have.

‣ Technically, selling is what you do once you are in front of a prospective client. Selling can also be thought of as a conversation (where the topic is "The Possibility of Doing Business") and a sorting process (you're merely sorting the yes's from the no's). Finally, selling is an examination; a test of a prospective client's ability to do business with you. Note that none of these definitions require you to change your personality in order to sell more business; it's important that you be yourself in a selling situation. However, you must also learn and follow an organized selling system in order to get the best results.

4

The Three Biggest Mistakes Professional Service Providers Make—and the Easy Way To Avoid These Costly Blunders

Over the years, I have observed the mistakes of many professional service providers in selling situations; that is, in situations where they were trying to acquire a new client or engagement. Let's examine the three most common and critical errors professionals tend to make when selling. If you can learn to avoid these errors, your sales effectiveness will improve dramatically—your closing ratio should skyrocket to almost 100 percent.

Mistake 1: They Don't Know When the Sale Is Made

Ever talk yourself out of a sale? Have you walked out of a selling situation thinking you had a new client, but nothing ever transpired? Who hasn't?

Here's the single biggest mistake professionals make in the selling situation: They don't know when the sale is made, and they either neglect to secure a decision from the client or they keep gabbing and wind up talking themselves out of a sale.

Professionals who wouldn't dream of approaching a project or task without a work plan, find themselves ad-libbing or going with the flow to make the sale. They allow the prospect to control the selling process. They often leave the sales interview without knowing where they are because they don't know where they've been and have no clue as to what the next step is to get the engagement.

Following a specific systematic sequence and controlling the steps through this process is vital to your success in acquiring new clients and getting more business from existing ones.

Selling is a matter of timing. Prospective clients have to be "closed"; that is, agreements have to be finalized when the prospective clients are positive and most inclined to do so. If the engagement is not secured, even by a handshake, when the prospective client is positive, there is only one way they can swing when you leave: negative.

Utilizing a systematic approach to selling and conducting a sales examination is critical. It will tell you where you are in the sales process and inform you if and when to close the sale or secure commitments.

Mistake 2: They Assume Answers Rather Than Ask Questions

Today's professionals seem to have the solution to every business problem. In fact, many firms no longer merely offer plain old consulting or other professional services but instead are in the business of "providing business solutions."

Unfortunately, most professionals monopolize the precious time they have in front of a prospective client with their repartee, often only allowing the prospect to listen (whether or not it's interesting). I've seen many professionals try to tell the prospective client the solution before they have adequately diagnosed the problem.

Professionals need to ask many more questions to ensure a complete understanding of the prospect's perspective. They need to take the conversation out of the intellectual and into the emotional, because people buy for emotional reasons first and then justify their decisions intellectually (more on this in Chapter 7). If other professionals were held liable for their solutions as often as physicians are, liability insurance premiums would skyrocket!

In selling professional services, people buy other people. Also, prospective clients care less about what you have to say compared to what they have to say. This may not be your opinion on the subject.

You may believe that the more information and expertise you bestow on prospective clients, the more likely they are to buy. Although this might be true at times when dealing with other consultants and professionals, it is definitely not true most of the time when dealing with entrepreneurs and businesspeople. They aren't interested in the endless details; they only want the job done right. The exception occurs when they are not true buyers after all, but merely interested in tapping your brain for free so they can give their existing service providers your great ideas.

There is a time and place to offer solutions, and it does not come early in the sales interview.

Mistake 3: They Plead for the Business And Often Wind Up Giving It Away Unnecessarily

Do all prospective clients buy strictly on price? As hard as it is to believe, even in today's difficult economic climate with competition never greater, more people than you think buy the service that is not the cheapest.

Many service providers, usually because they aren't very successful at selling, often find themselves hoping, wishing, and even begging for the opportunity to just show their expertise and then maybe make a sale. Some even do this by offering free engagements.

This is unlike the highly successful professional who views her time as extremely valuable, is confident in her firm's ability to do the work, and is not interested in every prospective client that comes along. The best business developers in the professions are selective about who they do business with and the type of work they do—even when business is down. They realize their services have merit and expect to be paid in accordance with that value. This attitude does not come from being successful but rather causes success—because people like doing business with people who are successful. Prospective clients often back away from the service-provider who needs the business so badly that he cuts fees over and over again.

The Physician as Role Model

I had a difficult time accepting the role of salesperson for professional services. For some reason, selling has always been unpleasant to me.

I certainly don't like salespeople in general, nor being pressured, told what to do, or "sold."

I do find that I like helping people and "prescribing" answers to their concerns. Therefore, I adopted the physician as a role model. In order to be more successful at selling professional services, and to ease the pain and suffering of failure and rejection, start looking at yourself as a "business doctor" (see Exhibit 3).

Do doctors look like salespeople? Do they act like salespeople? Do they give presentations? How would you feel, and what would you do, if your doctor started selling you? Probably leave!

That's one of the beauties of this analogy. Many doctors are highly successful at selling additional services to their existing patients and to new patients without looking, acting, or sounding like

Exhibit 3. The physician as role model.

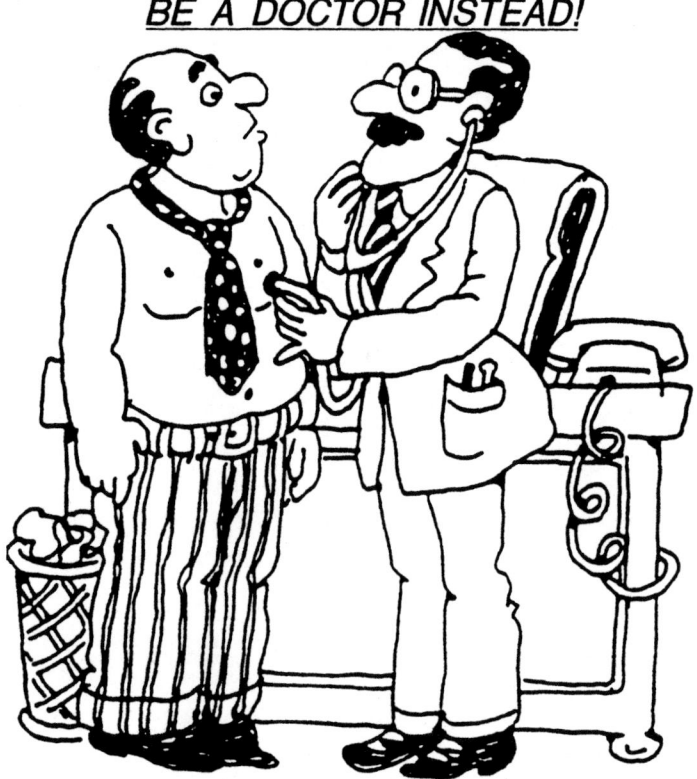

NEVER SELL......
BE A DOCTOR INSTEAD!

salespeople. That's what aids their credibility! They are low-key and nonthreatening. They ask questions, perform tests, and prescribe solutions.

But the patient comes to them, you say? Some of us remember when doctors still made house calls. And you or your firm have had prospective and current clients visit your office who still weren't sold.

Do you go to the cheapest doctor in town? Of course not! Then why do we expect clients to beat us up on fees? If we approach the client relationship correctly, we are their business doctors. Many of your clients feel their business is their baby that sometimes takes precedence over their family and their personal health. So why shouldn't they pay accordingly?

The first sale you have to make is to yourself. There is something about the medical profession, the legal profession, and the respective learning programs and processes that imbue physicians and attorneys with the philosophy that "I am worth it! My services are valuable!" Most of us weren't mentally prepared like that in school.

You will never be paid more than what you think you are worth.

Avoiding the Pain and Suffering of Rejection

We can use physicians as a role models in helping us sell more effectively by being detached emotionally from the sales process. To be more successful at selling, you have to guard your self-esteem judiciously. You must keep your spirits up, or you won't be successful.

The good physician has a caring-but-detached attitude toward her patients. Sure, she wants her patients to be well; it's part of her professional pride. And her patients will speak highly of her when she cures them. But do you think doctors spend a lot of time worrying and beating themselves up when their patients don't follow their recommendation or "buy"? Of course not—they'd go bananas. This may explain why there is a high incidence of suicide among psychiatrists— those who can't remain detached become depressed and unhappy, too.

Detachment is a very valuable lesson you can learn from doctors. If your client is "well"—if he doesn't think he has a problem—no matter how often you tell him what his problem is or how convincingly through eloquent presentations, he won't take action. If he does not feel the hurt himself, nothing can happen.

All you can do is be a good business doctor and perform your examinations and tests to the best of your ability. This attitude will make selling much easier, increase your closing percentage, and allow you to charge and receive higher fees.

Diagnosis and Rx 1: For Healthy Sales, Avoid These Three Mistakes

▸ Mistake 1: They don't know when the sale is made. Many professionals don't realize when the sale is made. So, they either leave the selling situation before getting a commitment or they keep on blabbing away and talk themselves out of a sale.

This mistake can be prevented if you go into a selling situation with a systematic plan that details what should occur at each step of the process. Since selling is a matter of timing, agreements must be finalized when the prospective clients are most inclined to do so. If you use the sales examination prescribed in this book each time you attempt a sale, you'll know exactly what needs to happen and when it needs to happen. Using this plan, you'll always know if and when to close the prospect. (Chapter 5 details one such sales plan).

▸ Mistake 2: They assume answers rather than ask questions. Today's professionals seem to have the solution to every business problem, and they want to share it with the prospective client as soon as possible—often before they've actually taken the time to discover the real issues involved.

To sell more business, you need to ask more questions. When you've secured an appointment with a potential client, don't monopolize the conversation by chattering on about what you know and your brilliant solutions to their problems. Instead, take the time to ask questions and really listen to what the prospect has to say. Even if you were right in the first place about what was wrong, taking the time to listen to the prospect will provide you with much more information and improve your working relationship. There is a time and place to offer solutions, and it does not come early in the sales interview.

▸ Mistake 3: They plead for the business and often wind up giving it away unnecessarily. You may find this hard to believe, but many prospective clients do not buy strictly on price. If they see superior benefits in working with you, they will pay more for your services.

The top producers in the professions are selective about who they do business with. They realize their services have merit and expect to be paid accordingly. This attitude is attractive to prospective clients—they prefer to work with someone who is already successful.

Don't make a habit of cutting your fees to attract more clients. By lowering your prices, you are taking value away from your work. Instead, focus on making your services more valuable and unique to the prospective client; maintain an attitude that you don't *need* the business (you'd like the business on appropriate terms, but you don't *need* to get it in order to survive). By the way, even if you do need the business, having an attitude of success will serve you better than an appearance that you're begging for business (which person would you rather buy from?)

Diagnosis and Rx 2: Act Like a Doctor and Be Cured

- Doctors are good role models for successfully selling professional services because they are highly successful at selling additional services to new and existing patients without ever looking, acting, or sounding like salespeople. They are low-key and nonthreatening and have tremendous credibility.

  Think about your last doctor visit. How did the physician talk to you? Did you end up buying more than you thought in the way of products (x-rays, tests) or services (additional visits, therapy)? Did you feel like you were being sold?
- You may feel more comfortable with "prescribing" than selling. Like doctors helping their patients, service-providers are in the business of fixing problems and eliminating pain (the prospect's mental anguish and stress). Think of yourself as a doctor next time you're in a selling situation, and conduct your "patient interview" accordingly. Just like doctors, we are experienced at performing tests, diagnosing problems and concerns, and offering solutions. But—like a doctor who fears malpractice—remember not to prescribe any solutions until you've heard everything the customers have to say and are sure, based on their explanation, that you understand what the real problems are.
- Doctors have the right perspective on fees: They truly believe their services are valuable and that they should be paid accordingly. Act like a successful person, and you will be treated like one. Be confident about your abilities, and project this confidence to the people you meet. Remember: You will never be paid more than what you think you are worth.

▸ Physicians have a caring-but-detached attitude toward the selling process. You can sell more effectively and maintain a better attitude by being detached emotionally from the sales process. When doctors give advice, they hope patients will follow it. However, if the patients don't, the physician can't worry about it. If patient X doesn't quit smoking, his doctor isn't going to take that as a personal insult. The doctor gave his best advice; it's up to the patient to follow it.

You should apply this caring-but-detached attitude to your sales as well. In selling, you truly want to offer your clients and prospects the best services. But, if they turn you down, you can't take it personally; it has very little to do with you and a lot to do with them.

Part Two

The Sales Examination

5

Conducting a Sales Examination: The Six Diagnostic Tests To Determine Whether A Client Is Sold 90 Percent Of the Time

On the first day I worked in public accounting, when I arrived at the client's location, the manager on the job reviewed his audit program with me. An audit program is a series of tasks, examinations, and tests performed in a certain order to produce a specific result. This systematic process put the manager in control of the engagement.

When I first started selling professional services, I practiced a somewhat haphazard process. Basically, I tried to get people to like me, I asked a few questions, told them what I did and how it could help them, and I asked them (sometimes, when I wasn't afraid) to engage my services. Then, I would be hit by all sorts of stalls and objections ("Your fees are too high," and so on). I felt that the sales process was totally out of control, and I wasn't very successful at securing new clients. I was depressed.

But, being the good auditor that I was, I analyzed each sales call by reviewing what went wrong, what was missing, and what was said (or not said). My first discovery was that I was lacking many elements of a successful sale because I forgot to cover certain important items, like fees or the decision-making process. Maybe you've had a similar experience after a sales interview: "Gosh, I forgot to ask them when they'd planned on doing something!"

As an accountant, I hated to make mistakes or be out of control. I realized that if I conducted each sales interview following an outline of all of the important points that needed to be covered, I might be more successful at selling. And, if I discovered and addressed those stalls and objections (reasons for not doing business) early on in the process, I could save myself a lot of time and grief. So, I decided to write an action plan that I would follow every time I was in front of a prospective client.

Was I surprised! The very first time I followed the plan, covering all of the important bases, I secured a new client! Using this approach, my closing ratio quickly zoomed to 70 percent of the people I interviewed, to over 90 percent of the people that passed some of my tests.

As I monitored my sales progress, I noticed that people would not become my clients unless they had certain characteristics, unless they passed certain tests. Those people who didn't become my clients failed the tests and therefore didn't "qualify" to be my clients. No matter what I did, be it elaborate formal presentations, articulate and detailed proposals, lobbying, or follow-up, if the prospective client couldn't or wouldn't pass my sales tests, I wouldn't get hired. And whether I was engaged or not had little to do with me and more to do with the prospective client (thereby removing the feelings of failure and rejection). Thus, the sales examination was born. I hope you will utilize the tests described below in every selling situation.

The Sales Examination

The following is an overview of the steps needed to conduct a sales audit. Detailed instructions for each step are in ensuing chapters. If you perform the audit to the best of your abilities, and your prospective client passes the examination, you will have a sale approximately 90 percent of the time:

Step 1: Test for Personal Chemistry
Step 2: Test for Emotional Needs, Wants, Desires, or Musts
Step 3: Test for Commitment to Action
Step 4: Test for Ability and Desire to Pay
Step 5: Test for Knowledge of the Decision Making Process and the Ability to Influence That Process
Step 6: Test to See If a Presentation or a Proposal Is Necessary, and Determine What It Should Look Like

If the prospective client passes these tests, we are then in a position to go to the final two steps:

Step 7: Prepare a Custom-Designed Presentation and/or Proposal
Step 8: Finalize the Agreement

How the Steps Must Progress

In this systematic selling plan, each step must be completed in order. If a step does not go well, it may be your cue to cease that sales examination and go on to the next prospect.

Fulfilling Step 1: Test for Personal Chemistry

To fulfill the first step, you need to have good personal chemistry with the buyer. Few sales of intangible professional services are made when buyers and sellers don't hit it off. The client wants someone she can relate to, feel comfortable with, and even like.

Conversely, the physical item itself drives the sale of a tangible piece. You could be madly in love with the car salesperson, but if he doesn't have what you want on the lot or can't get it, you'll go someplace else.

If you can't achieve good chemistry with the prospective client, you may as well save your time and stop the sales call right there. And that's okay; nobody hits it off with everybody. It may be wise at that point to turn that person over to someone else who may be able to develop a relationship with the prospect. Usually, however, if you follow the methods of establishing chemistry as taught in this book (learned from the top business producers in all of the professions), you will hit it off with the vast majority of buyers most of the time. In the last fourteen years of selling in this manner, I've only failed to develop some kind of chemistry five times—out of approximately 1,500 sales interviews.

Please remember that chemistry can be as much as 50 to 80 percent of making the sale. You can be the greatest technical genius in the entire world of your profession, win the Nobel Prize, be published in an appendix to the Bible, but if people don't feel comfortable or like you, you still won't get the business.

Reaching Step 2: Test for Emotional Needs, Wants, Desires, Or Musts

Once you have achieved a good chemistry with the prospective client, you need to proceed to second base. I call all of the needs, wants, desires, or musts "hurts" or "aches," because those are what a physician would be testing for.

Most salespeople never find out where it hurts. They're looking for "hot buttons" or some other such nonsense; these things exist only on the surface. You'll be searching a little deeper, under the skin. In Chapter 7, I'll show you specific ways to find out where it hurts. I've never read another book or listened to a tape that explains how to do this specifically and diagnostically. In order for you to proceed, these emotional needs, wants, desires and musts have to exist in the buyer.

Step 3: Test for Commitment to Action

But you must also attain Step 3, because some people who have hurts are merely complainers. You'll learn how to do that in Chapters 7 and 8.

If your prospective buyer doesn't have any hurts and/or they aren't committed to action, you should stop the sales call—and that's okay, because nobody sells everybody.

I've discovered that these first three steps really drive the entire sale. If you can truly grasp and administer these steps, your closing ratio will skyrocket. And Steps 2 and 3 propel the remaining six steps—if they are applied effectively.

Getting to Step 4: Test for Ability and Desire to Pay

Once you are satisfied that the patient does indeed have symptoms that need to be treated, and that they want to be cured, you can advance to Step 4. The time to test for money is right after you find out where it hurts. People have a totally different capacity for listening to "what it's going to cost" when they've realized what their hurts are and know that they want to fix them. Stalls and objections vanish into the air when you discuss fees at this point in the sales call.

If the prospective client doesn't pass this test, you should end the sales call.

Closing the Sale: Steps 5 and 6

In order to get the business, you have to cover Step 5: Test for Knowledge of the Decision-Making Process and the Ability to Influence that Process and Step 6: Test to See If a Presentation or a Proposal Is Necessary, and Determine What It Should Look Like.

Unfortunately, so many sales have been lost that should have been won because these two areas were not handled effectively. I'll show you how to so thoroughly test these steps, that you will have an advantage over the competition that no one will ever take away.

Completing the Process: Steps 7 and 8

After you have completed these steps, my experience, and that of thousands of people I've trained, is that you will have a sale over 90 percent of the time.

The remaining two steps—Step 7: Prepare a Customized Presentation and/or Proposal and Step 8: Finalize the Agreement—are the easiest parts of the sale, if you have conducted the first six steps thoroughly and accurately. I'll show you everything I've learned that's been proved to work in selling professional services in order to help you do that.

The Advantages of the Sales Examination Over Conventional Techniques

Here's what conducting a sales examination accomplishes for you:

- Turns a sales call into an interview
- Gives you control of the sales process
- Avoids time-wasting traps
- Decreases the likelihood of being used as a reference library or free consultant
- Removes the pain and suffering of failure and rejection
- Differentiates your behavior from that of your competition
- Involves the client emotionally
- Transmits to the prospective client the behavior and attitude of a caring professional
- Provides a thorough analysis of the client's problems, needs, wants, and desires, which then enables you to provide the best prescriptions

- Eliminates bottlenecks, stalls, and objections early in the sales process
- Helps you make a presentation and/or proposal, when necessary, that is customized for the situation and thus more likely to succeed
- Removes pressure from you as seller
- Makes prospect feel at ease because he is being interviewed, not sold
- Establishes timing of presentation when people are most willing to listen and act
- Gives you a track to follow to avoid mistakes
- Uses the seller decision points to determine if it makes sense to stay in the sales process
- Gains commitment as the process continues and makes closing seem natural
- Leads more clients to close themselves

Diagnosis and Rx: Use this Eight-Step Workout to Help You Grow Your Business

To achieve maximum business development results, you must follow this plan, step by step. If at any time, you find that you cannot complete a step, stop the sales call. Detailed instructions for each step are in ensuing chapters. If you fulfill these steps to the best of your ability, and your prospective client passes the examination, you will have a sale approximately 90% of the time.

Step 1: Test for Personal Chemistry. Make sure that prospective clients feel at ease with you (one indication that they do is that you feel comfortable with them).

Step 2: Test for Emotional Needs, Wants, Desires, or Musts. If your prospective clients don't have these underlying aches, they're not going to buy anything from you.

Step 3: Test for Commitment to Action. Your prospective buyers must have aches, but, if you want to make a sale, they must also be committed to doing something to cure them.

Step 4: Test for Ability and Desire to Pay. Even if your prospects have many problems *and* want to fix them, you must also make sure they have the money to pay your fees. If not, you're out of there.

Step 5: Test for Knowledge of the Decision-Making Process and the Ability to Influence that Process. After you've found aches, commitment, and money, you still need to find out exactly who will make the decision to hire you, and then do your best to contact the decision-makers and control the process.

Step 6: Test to See if a Presentation or a Proposal Is Necessary, and Determine What It Should Look Like. Sometimes presentations and proposals are necessary. If so, you must have the prospect tell you exactly what these items should look like in order for you to get the sale.

If you are able to reach Step 6, you can then choose to proceed to the final two steps:

Step 7: Prepare a Custom-Designed Presentation and/or Proposal. If you have successfully taken the prospect through the first six steps and he or she wants a presentation or proposal, you must now create a custom-designed piece—if you want the business.

Step 8: Finalize the Agreement. In this last step, you need to resolve all the relevant issues, such as when the work will begin, payment schedule, and so on.

6

Testing for Positive Chemical Reaction

In order to sell more business, you must be adept at testing for and creating a good relationship with prospective clients. Therefore, it's critical for you to know how to test for chemistry, improve chemistry, and even create chemistry where it does not automatically exist. This is Step 1 of the sales examination. You'll need to conduct this test and improve chemistry from the moment you meet someone through the close of the sale.

Why Chemistry Is Important to Successful Selling

Selling intangible services is more difficult than selling tangible products. If you go to purchase an automobile, a computer, or a house, your desire for the tangible item will override any lack of personal chemistry you have with the salesperson. A buyer is unlikely to turn down a good deal on a computer just because she doesn't like the salesperson.

But, in selling intangible services, the prospective client is buying *you*. Very few people will hire professional service providers whom they don't like or don't feel comfortable with. That's one of their tests in deciding whom to hire: "Can I get along with this person? Will he fit in well with my staff? Do I like him?"

Improve chemistry and conduct a thorough examination of this step in order to:

1. *Create special feelings for you.* Many of us have lost sales to competitors who were probably less qualified to do the work than we were. If personal chemistry is weak or lacking, it is almost impossible

to make the sale. On the other hand, prospective clients often will go out of their way to hire you if they like you.

By testing for and then creating special feelings for us, we can separate ourselves from competition who may not give this subject much thought or effort. Also, clients are much more likely to refer business to and buy additional services from their professional service provider when chemistry exists. Strong personal chemistry can be 50 to 80 percent of making the sale.

2. *Have people feel comfortable with you and open up to you.* It's imperative as business doctors that we have the prospective client (the patient) tell us what is *really* bothering them rather than give some superficial reason for discussion.

Very often professionals walk into a selling situation where the prospective client is just looking. You've heard perfunctory statements like this before: "We're considering doing something . . ." or "We decided it was time to review our professional relationships. . . ."

Just like a physician, we need to conduct a thorough examination of the client in order to prescribe correctly. To do that, prospective clients must feel comfortable with us. Without good personal chemistry, this will not happen.

3. *Have them trust and respect you as one of their own.* Think about where you live, what kind of car you drive, how you dress, what your hairstyle looks like, how long your sideburns are. Human beings have a very basic desire to fit in. We tend to trust people much more quickly if they are very similar to us. Do you wear leisure suits to work? What color shirt do you wear? What length is your skirt? Do you dress conservatively or a bit on the wild side?

The same holds true for our prospective clients. Although we may not dress like our clients, chances are we share many of the same beliefs, goals, and morals. Having people trust you is tantamount to getting hired. Without solid personal chemistry, trust cannot exist.

4. *Test for and create an equal adult relationship.* Ever feel like some of your clients look down on you? Do you look down on some of them? Our clients should see us as equals. Then it is more likely they will respect us and treat us the way we want to be regarded. And they will be more likely to abide by our prescriptions and pay our fees!

5. *Make sure they never see you as selling something.* We never want the prospective client to feel as if you are trying to sell them something, because that creates fear, distancing, and distrust. Anytime someone perceives they are being sold, they will put up psychological

and even physical barriers to the sales process. For example, most people are scared to walk into auto dealerships for fear of being taken advantage of. By using the physician approach and adopting the behavior almost the exact opposite of what one would expect from a salesperson, you will get by these barriers. And people will tell you just how to sell them during the sales examination.

How to Create Personal Chemistry

Some people are naturals at having people like them and feel comfortable with others from the get-go. These are the same people who were popular in high school. Unfortunately, the rest of us have to work at it. Following are some proven ways, which I've learned from the top business products in the professions, to create personal chemistry.

Clear the Decks

It's almost impossible to get someone's attention and build personal chemistry if there are distractions. Those who have attempted to conduct business where the prospective client is interrupted by a secretary, is busy answering calls, or is upset or indisposed because of a problem will know exactly how difficult this is.

People tend to act very differently and are more prone to open up to us once they are off their "throne." Also, prospective clients are much less likely to open up to us in their offices because "the walls have ears." Therefore, it is imperative to create a selling situation where there will be no distractions; in this way, you'll set the correct ambiance for a productive meeting.

The best time to conduct a sales interview, especially an initial meeting, is over lunch. There is something special about a relaxed atmosphere away from the office that gives prospective clients the opportunity to open up and share their true concerns and desires. Sure, there are distractions in a restaurant, but they are temporary and unimportant to the buyer.

You can establish the best location for the sales interview when you make the appointment over the phone. Ask the prospective clients when they would like to meet for lunch to discuss their situation.

Why conduct meetings at lunch? Generally, it is the one time of your day that is open. And the same holds true for your future clients. Give them the courtesy of not taking too much time away from their work. Everybody likes to be treated to lunch. Beware: The prospective client who is too busy or uninterested in meeting for lunch may not be a buyer after all. And eating is a social occasion—it makes for a more relaxed atmosphere. Also, if people are hungry, there's no way you'll be able to capture and keep their attention throughout the sales process.

Some professionals don't want to spend the money taking a client to lunch. But remember, you don't have to dine at the most expensive restaurant in town; the best place for a meeting may be near the client's office. I look at lunches as a vital investment and an inexpensive way to rent an office for an hour. But, you say, shouldn't you want to see their manufacturing plant and/or offices to show your interest in them? Sure, but do so before or after lunch. If you cannot get the prospective client out of the building for lunch or coffee, seek to commandeer a conference room on their premises.

Remember, serious and smart buyers want your undivided attention, too. Setting up the wrong environment for a sales meeting will hurt the end result. And chances are your competition hasn't thought of it; this is one more way to distinguish yourself from them.

Start at the Beginning

If you are so fortunate as to be referred into a sales interview from a client or other source (banker, attorney, insurance person), mention that connection at the start of the meeting to refresh the buyer's mind and secure his attention.

Say something like, "It was nice of Sue Jones to bring us together. Did she happen to tell you anything about us when she made the referral or why she referred us?"

This question reestablishes how you and the buyer have come together. There are three answers to this question, all of which are okay, because, at the very least, we have gained their attention:

1. "No."
2. "Yes, but I've forgotten."
3. "Yes. She mentioned that you are the engineers on several of her projects, and that you had a great deal of experience with situations like ours." (Or something like that.)

It is worth asking the question just for the possibility of response number three. With this response, the sales interview starts off on the best foot.

Engage in Small Talk—But Be Careful!

Everyone knows that small talk can be a good way to break the ice with a prospective client—if one is good at it and the buyer is receptive. But be careful: My experience is that you have about eight seconds to capture the prospective client's interest and attention. Talking about the weather, last night's football game, something unique about their office, or the sailfish on the wall can create anxiety rather than relieve it. In today's hurried world, many people simply don't have the time or temperament to chitchat for twenty minutes about nothing. And sometimes this innocuous chatter can carry on throughout the entire sales interview without anything being accomplished.

If you are already talented at this art, by all means keep employing it. If you're not, take the other person's lead. If they start small talk with you, by all means engage with them or you'll appear arrogant.

The Eight-Year-Old's Approach

In order to master a given skill, you must look to learn from anyplace you can. Fortunately for you, the great majority of your competition have their eyes, ears, and minds shut to being masterful, or even competent, at creating chemistry. This method was taught to me by an eight-year-old girl, who obviously knew a heck of a lot more about the subject than I did!

I was at a friend's house for a barbecue, when his daughter walked up to me and said, "When I grow up, I want to marry someone just like you." Wow—I don't get those kinds of compliments every day. Here, kid, take my wallet. Whatever you want that I have is now yours. I want to make you the beneficiary of my entire estate!

The lesson to be learned in creating chemistry is, if the opportunity presents itself, tell someone something you know they absolutely want to hear. Sadly, most salespeople abuse this idea and march into the buyer's office and proclaims something like, "Oooh . . . is that your bowling trophy, sir? Are you really a bowler? Wow!" Or "What beautiful offices you have." How many times have you heard that before?

No, this message must come from your heart—you have to really mean it and say it with emotion. One of the nicest pieces of business I ever sold was assuredly closed when I told the founding partner, "I bet you had more than a few sleepless nights building this business by yourself."

Employ Active and Empathetic Listening

Abraham Lincoln said, "People don't care how much you know, until they know how much you care." Good old Abe knew human beings, all right. He understood that people wouldn't pay attention to your prescriptions, solutions, advice, or credentials unless they knew you were truly concerned about them.

I've left the most successful method of establishing chemistry for last. People will fall in love with you if you listen to them! I use the term *listening* in this context to embrace a certain connotation. Here, listening means to interact with someone so they get the feeling that you truly care about them and that what they say is important to you.

Clients want professional service providers who will listen to them; people care much more about what they have to say than what you have to say. Unfortunately, they rarely find themselves in front of someone willing to listen without interruption. This need to be listened to is so vital that some people utilize the services of psychiatrists (and pay a dandy sum doing so) just to have someone attend to their concerns. And no matter how young you were, no matter how strong the sexual attraction was way back when, you never would have married your spouse if he or she hadn't listened to you! Does your best friend listen to you? Of course, otherwise he or she would not be your best friend!

If you can tune up your listening skills, you will sell more work, have better relationships with your clients and referral sources, and totally separate yourself from the competition. Fee objections, too, will not be as prominent.

One of my CPA clients had problems for many years with one of his clients about fees. The CPA's client was almost brutal about yearly fee reductions. He asked me what to do, because the annual audit was coming to a close and he would soon have to sit down with the client and negotiate adjustments and fees.

I suggested that he take his client out to lunch and say hardly a word; just give the client the opportunity to let off some steam and find out why he was always so concerned about paying too much. What was the real problem anyway?

It turned out that the CPA's client was Japanese. By keeping his mouth shut, the CPA learned that his client saw it as his duty to bargain over fees as a matter of honor to his company. There was nothing wrong with the services rendered; in fact, the client was delighted with the timeliness and professionalism of the CPA over the years. What was lacking was a relationship between the two, which was established that day by allowing the client to talk at length about his job, his career, and his concerns. When the meeting was drawing to a close, the CPA asked his client what to do about fees. His client said no adjustment was necessary!

Surprised? Don't be. As in all other professions, the rainmakers in the accounting profession regularly charge higher fees than their competitors and have a higher realization than their associates because they are giving their clients something they want: a CPA who truly cares about them and their business and who does much more than just drop off or mail the financials once a quarter.

Another client of mine (Lou, a phenomenally successful consultant) had been trying to secure a particular client for eight years. Every time they got together, Lou could never close the deal. Finally, after two days of my training with his firm, Lou decided to take the guy out to lunch. He called me immediately afterward with the good news—Lou had secured his business right then and there in the restaurant.

Listening is critical from a control standpoint as well. Many people think that the talker controls the selling situation. Not true; the talker dominates the conversation, but the listener or interviewer directs the meeting. Watch *60 Minutes* some Sunday evening, and you'll see what I mean!

The Twelve Keys to Active and Empathetic Listening

Here's how to become much better at the skill of listening.

1. Always Take Written Notes

What does it say about someone who takes written notes during a sales interview? Doesn't it say that he is concerned, effective, and organized? Won't the buyer get the feeling that what he is saying is important (and that he, too, is important)?

Many of us try to communicate these qualities to the prospective client with our banter. It is much more effective if the buyer perceives them himself by noticing our actions. I generally ask the buyer's permission before I start taking notes; this puts them at ease. It also reinforces the fact that what they are telling me is very important.

Written notes also provide the evidence, details, and history we need to refer to in the process of securing a client; this data simply cannot be remembered. So, don't be afraid to take notes—in over 1,500 sales calls, no one has ever asked me not to.

2. Never Interrupt the Client

People love to talk and talk. . . . Unfortunately, most professionals are in too much of a hurry to stop and listen. Chances are, however, that no one else in the client's life listens, either.

Never interrupt anyone in a selling interview—except in case of fire or nuclear attack. If the prospective client babbles on and strays off the subject, you can always direct him back with a question. How do you feel when you're interrupted? Rainmakers often close many more sales than their competitors by simply listening more and interrupting less than the competition does.

3. Give Verbal and Visual Signals

Too basic, you say? I've been on dozens of sales interviews, observing professional service providers who sit blank-faced.

You must let the buyer know that they are being listened to or they will stop talking. Nod your head, say things like "I see" or "Uh-huh" to let the buyer know you are on-line with their spoken thoughts.

4. Presume and Act As if Whatever the Prospective Client Says Is Important

Sometimes you have to pretend that what the buyer says is important, because you may have had a hundred clients in the same exact situation and heard the same concerns expressed before. However, these are special issues to the buyer, and they will be disappointed unless you hear them out.

5. Don't Think

Write down thoughts and questions that come to you. If you spend time thinking, you are not listening—and the buyer will know that.

It is inevitable that thoughts and more questions come to you while listening. Great! That will be a good way to keep the conversation going when the buyer stops talking. Merely note these thoughts and questions on the paper where you are taking notes.

6. *Deal with Imprecise Words*

Some people make statements such as they are "fairly pleased" with their current provider or situation or "The fees are too high" or "We're not getting the kind of service we want." What do these words and statements mean? Heck if I know.

In order to be a better listener (and a better seller), find out immediately. Don't let inexact words or statements pass you by, or you won't find out what the buyer's true motives are or diagnose the situation correctly.

Don't be a mind reader! Say something like, "When you said that you were fairly pleased with your current attorney, what did that mean?" or "Why do you say that her fees are too high—is it because of lack of service or something else?" or "Can you expand or give me an example of what you mean by 'not getting the kind of service you want?' "

Afraid to pursue vague statements or words? Don't be. The buyer often does not realize what she has said. And we were all taught from childhood to redefine our assertions.

In fourteen years of asking people to expand upon what they have said, no one has ever refused me. If they ever did, it would indicate a lack of personal chemistry.

7. *Be Curious*

Remember the time before you started kindergarten? If not, how about before your children started school? Preschool-age children are very curious about everything. "Oh, Daddy, look at the truck!" As we get older, we tend to stop noticing things.

However, prospective and existing clients love it when others are curious about them and their jobs, interests, and lives. Too few others in their lives show much of an interest.

Be like that little child when you meet with the client and walk into their plant or office. Let your curiosity take over. People will be much more apt to like you, be open and honest with you, and be comfortable.

8. *Leave Your Brochures in the Office*

No matter how much your firm has invested in its fancy brochure, chances are it looks and reads like everyone else's. I bet your brochure has pictures of professionals in it, appearing as if they are doing work. Or perhaps, pictures of your office. And it says that you are much more than mere consultants, architects, designers, or whatever; rather, you are business experts providing solutions based on the network of resources you have at your fingertips, blah, blah, blah.

Worse, some professionals often expect the brochure to do the selling for them. People don't buy professional services from brochures. Don't detract in any way from the interview: If you have a brochure handy, the buyer will start reading and quizzing you on it, thus taking control of the interview. So, leave the brochures at your office.

Brochures are somewhat necessary today only because everyone else has one. They provide an excellent accompaniment to a personal thank-you note sent immediately after the interview—which provides one more exposure for you. People love personal thank-you notes, and your competition won't take the time to write them.

9. Hold Yourself Back

Professional service providers think they are supposed to offer solutions immediately when they hear a concern from the buyer. This is not how doctors and many of the best business generators in the professions sell.

There is a time and place to offer solutions. It is not when you hear a hot button; it is later in the selling interview after all of the buyer's needs, wants, desires, and musts are on the table. If you start answering concerns as you hear them, you will be doing far too much talking and will interrupt the good flow that the buyer is feeling.

Worse, you'll sound just like salespeople and your competition. Ever have conversation like this?

The buyer: We aren't receiving our financial statements on time from our current CPA.

The CPA: No problem! We'll get you the financials when you want them!

The buyer: That's what our last CPA said.

Remember, what you say about yourself is your opinion and carries little weight. Wait until the appropriate time to answer all of the buyer's concerns (covered in Chapter 10).

10. Be Yourself

Some professionals adopt another persona when they meet with prospective clients. They start acting like they think they're supposed to—as if they were on a first date.

Let the buyer meet the real you. Be open and vulnerable; be your-self. If they hire you but never meet the real you until afterward and don't like you, they'll hire someone else anyway. It's only by being open yourself that others can be accessible to you.

11. Don't Answer Unasked Questions

People do not buy firms, they buy individuals. Don't answer a lot of *unasked* questions about your firm. I've seen people go into a long dissertation about when their firm was founded, how many profes-sionals they have, blah, blah, blah.

Buyers couldn't care less. They care about getting their needs, wants, desires, and musts met. If you have to say something about your firm and your experience, make it short and sweet. The best time to discuss your firm and qualifications is in Step 6 (see Chapter 10).

12. Use "Expanders"

Psychotherapists have ways of encouraging people to open up. Next time you're in the shrink's office or even your regular physician's or dentist's office, pay attention to how they keep you talking. Smart doctors use words that act as a stimulus for the patient to amplify and develop his or her thoughts and statements. They are looking for the causes of the problems, so that they can offer the correct solutions or prescriptions.

Your goal, as a seller of professional services, is to get people talking about their situation as much as possible. In over 1,500 sales calls these past fourteen years, I've learned that there is a direct rela-tionship between the amount that people talk and the likelihood of their hiring you.

Here are some of the expanders I've learned, and successfully used, over the years. I've included as examples real responses to the expanders on my own sales interviews and those I've attended with clients using this technique. Notice how expanders turn short or even one-word answers into valuable explanations and hurts:

A. "Because . . . ?"

Buyer: We use three different architectural firms for our buildings.
Architect: Because?
Buyer: We've never found one firm that can handle our range of projects.

Architect: Would you prefer to work with one firm, or doesn't it matter that you have to deal with all of these different people?

Buyer: We'd love to work with one firm—it would make our lives so much easier.

B. "Why is that?"

Consultant: Do you have a close working relationship with your consultants?

Buyer: Not really.

Consultant: Why is that?

Buyer: Gosh, we never found anyone that took a personal interest in us.

Graphic Designer: Is there anything you dislike about your current graphic design firm?

Buyer: Well, they could be coming up with some more original-looking materials. All of their stuff is starting to look the same.

Graphic Designer: Why is that?

Buyer: Most likely because they've had the same person on our account for years.

Graphic Designer: Have you talked to them about it?

Buyer: Sure. They say that they don't have anyone else available at this time.

Graphic Designer: Do you think that this situation has impacted your business in any way?

Buyer: Yes we do. We send a lot of direct mail. When the materials coming through the mail start looking all the same to our buyers, they ignore new products and special deals. We think it's cut into our response rate.

C. "And . . . ?"

Computer Consultant: How much turnaround time does it normally take for you to get back on-line with your current computer consultants?

Buyer: Normally they take about two to four hours to get here, and we're usually up and running within the day.

Computer Consultant: And . . . ?

Buyer: And they disrupt our entire operation. The people they have working for them have no experience in working with people, only machines. They're prima donnas and the whole department is upset by the time they're done.

D. "What happened?"

Attorney: How did Minton and Bore handle your most recent contract negotiations?
Buyer: Okay, I guess.
Attorney: What happened?
Buyer: We really had leverage on that deal, but they assigned one of their junior people to the negotiation. I really think we could have worked out a much better arrangement.
Attorney: And . . . ?
Buyer: And it cost us plenty in the end!

E. "Such as . . . ?"

Financial Consultant: Have you had any problems with the advice you're received from your current financial advisor?
Buyer: Yes.
Financial Consultant: Such as . . . ?
Buyer: Such as the time she told me it would be okay to co-sign a loan with my son. Yes, he wouldn't have been able to buy that new car he wanted, but then he wouldn't have been able to default on it either. I got stuck paying off a car that he couldn't afford in the first place, and he still owes me the money.

Building Chemistry with a Teammate

I strongly encourage team sales calls for establishing chemistry with prospective clients. Even if there is only one buyer, your chances increase by bringing someone else. If the buyer doesn't like you, it is possible he will like your associate. But don't bring the whole office.

Testing for personal chemistry on a joint sales call is quite simple: Watch to see who the conversation is being directed to. If you're asking the questions and the answers are going to your associate, she has the better chemistry and should take over.

In Chapter 11, we'll discuss the rules of team selling.

How to Test for Personal Chemistry

In this important step, you will have done all that you can to arrange for the best possible environment for a productive interview. You have tried your best to establish a positive chemistry with the prospective client.

Now you need to test this level of chemistry to decide how to proceed. If chemistry is sorely lacking, you can decide to terminate the sale or bring in others who will better interact with the client.

Don't forget, it's almost impossible to sell a prospective client if there isn't really good personal chemistry!

The test for personal chemistry is quite simple: How do you feel with the client? Are you comfortable with them?

Human emotions feed off each other. It's almost impossible to feel comfortable with someone who isn't comfortable with you. Do they like you? Ask yourself if you like them! If you feel put-off or distanced and are not particularly fond of them, guess what? They feel that way, too. However, if you feel comfortable with the buyers and like them, they've passed the first step.

Now you can proceed to Step 2: Test for Emotional Needs, Wants, Desires, or Musts.

Diagnosis and Rx: Achieve a Good pH Balance with Your Prospects

- ‣ Selling intangible services is very different from selling tangible products. When you sell services, the prospective client is buying *you*—you are integral to the sale. That is why personal chemistry is so important.
- ‣ In order to create personal chemistry, there are several things you must do. The first is to clear the decks; you need to create a selling situation where there are no distractions. The best place to do this is out of the prospect's office; ideally, you should take the prospect to lunch (or breakfast or dinner). If you can't get your prospects to leave the building, at least get them to leave their offices; ask them to reserve a conference room for your meeting.
- ‣ If you were referred to a prospect, mention that connection at the start of the meeting, to refresh the buyer's mind and secure his attention.
- ‣ Be careful about making small talk; it may make the prospect

uneasy. If you are already talented at this, keep doing it. If not, take the other person's lead: only engage in small talk if the buyer does first.

▸ One lesson to be learned in creating chemistry is that, if the opportunity presents itself and you're not at risk of appearing hokey or insincere, tell someone something you know he or she absolutely wants to hear. It's good to pay compliments, when they are genuine.

▸ You should spend most of your meeting listening to what the prospective client has to say.

▸ There are twelve keys to active listening which you should follow:

1. Always take written notes.
2. Never interrupt the client.
3. Give verbal and visual signals that show you're paying close attention.
4. Presume and act like whatever the prospective client says is important.
5. Don't think.
6. Deal with imprecise words.
7. Be curious.
8. Leave your brochures back at your office.
9. Hold yourself back from offering solutions.
10. Be yourself.
11. Don't answer unasked questions.
12. Use expanders to draw the prospect out. Expanders are phrases like "Because . . . ?" and "Why is that?"

▸ I encourage you to make team sales calls; they help in establishing chemistry, because a prospect may have better chemistry with one particular individual. You may want to go on a sales call with one or two very different co-workers, but don't bring the whole office. By the way, it's easy for you to tell who the prospect feels most comfortable with; it's whomever the prospect is directing the conversation to. If you're asking the questions and the answers are going to an associate, she has better chemistry and should take over.

7

Tender Loving Care: Satisfying Emotional Needs, Wants, Desires, and Musts

In this chapter, you will learn how to form a questioning strategy to discover the information necessary to correctly diagnose a prospective client. And you'll learn how to test the prospective clients for the emotional needs, wants, desires, and musts necessary to make a sale (Step 2 of the sales examination). This portion of the book teaches you the equivalence of how to conduct a physical examination on a patient.

Why People Buy

In order to sell effectively, you need to understand *why people buy.* An important selling rule to remember: People buy for emotional reasons and then justify their purchases intellectually.

The intent of any purchase can always be traced to the satisfaction of a highly emotional irritant (or irritants), whether a passionate need, want, desire, or something that must be done. To better accommodate the physician analogy, we can refer to these emotional causes as the buyer's hurts.

Therefore, the goal of Step 2 is to find out simply "Where does it hurt?" and to determine whether the patient is committed to becoming "well."

Selling Rule: If the patient is fine, and—despite your thorough examination—no emotional needs, wants, desires, or musts have been uncovered, a sale cannot be made.

We professional service providers have such high expectations of ourselves that we often "beat ourselves up" when a client isn't procured. This step diagnoses whether the client can be secured or not, whether the patient wants to and can be healed.

All of us have friends or relatives who should stop smoking or lose weight because these activities are endangering their health, but they refuse to do so. Does a physician lose much sleep when someone doesn't take his or her prescription? No; doctors are taught in medical school the concept of emotional detachment from their patients.

And so it is with some of our clients and prospective clients. Some have issues that should be confronted and solved, but, for whatever reason, they decide not to fix these things. Be a business doctor: don't be upset when someone doesn't take your prescription for success.

If you do a good job in conducting the diagnostic review in Step 2, if you have set the meeting up in the best possible environment for a free-flowing discussion, and if you have attempted to create a good personal chemistry with the prospective client, you can be very proud of that despite the results of the test. The rest is up to the patient.

Remember, you cannot convince anybody to do anything; they have to see it for themselves. People buy for their reasons, not yours. You will want to use a questioning strategy to elicit information, as well as the client's emotional needs, wants, and desires, in order to:

1. *Avoid wasting time.* Your time to market and sell is limited and, therefore, highly valuable. You don't want to invest this asset with people who have a low probability of buying. All too often professionals create proposals, thus giving away free ideas that are then turned over to the existing internal or external service provider. Or professionals do presentations for prospects who were really "suspects" with no intention of buying in the first place.

2. *Create special feelings for you.* People buy other people. Serious prospective clients like it when they finally find someone who is willing to listen to their concerns at length, without interruption.

3. *Separate yourself from the competition.* Chances are excellent that your competitors still sell the same way salespeople do. They will most likely conduct their interview in the buyer's office amidst dis-

tractions, ask a few questions, and then go into a lengthy dissertation about their firm and how brilliant and great they are.

The client will recognize the dramatically different approach you use as a "physician" versus the typical sales approach of your competition.

4. *Improve your client relationships by listening to their hurts.* Your relationships with many of your clients will improve as you pay more attention to them and listen more closely for the emotional issues they face.

An Example of the Hurt Analogy

Listen to the script of an interview I recently conducted with a new client ("Mr. Smith") at one of the CPA firms I consult with:

Allan: Thank you for agreeing to this interview. The purpose of our conversation is to discuss why you chose my client, XYZ & Co., as your new CPA firm. How long were you with your previous CPA firm?

Smith: About five years.

Allan: Was there any particular reason you can point to that caused you to change firms?

Smith: Oh yes. Their fees were way out of line.

Allan: In what way?

Smith: Well, I never really saw the person in charge of my account. Although they promised personalized service when we started with them, the only person I ever saw was a junior-level person who did the work.

Allan: How did you come to hire them in the first place?

Smith: Our bank had made some comments over the years about preferring to see a big-name firm on our financial reports. I wanted to keep them happy. So, I switched from the CPA I used to have to a very well known firm. But then I never saw anybody!

Allan: Would it have been important to interact with the partner in charge of your account?

Smith: Sure. Nobody ever sat down and explained these financial statements to me. I'm not an accountant; I run an auto dealership. Even if I was an accountant, I don't have the time to sit down and figure out what the heck is going on—I've got businesses to run and cars to sell. All they did was mail me the financials and my tax returns.

Allan: Is there any specific situation that you can look back on that caused you some problems because of this lack of contact?

Smith: I knew that business was down because of the economy and that I had more cars than I should've. What I didn't know was how bad my cash-flow situation really was and that my inventory was much, much higher than the previous year at the same time. I got late on some of my bills, and my vendors started screaming at me for cash. I went to my bank and all of a sudden they became real cautious about lending money because of the bank crisis, and I couldn't get more credit to stay on the good side of my vendors. A lot of good changing CPAs did me.

I had a lot of sleepless nights, I'll tell you. Almost couldn't meet payroll one week. I wound up taking a bath on most of my inventory just to generate some cash. Thank goodness we squeezed through! But that was the last straw with those other accountants; I was relying on them. If I just could have known how serious things really were, I would have taken some precautionary measures before things got so bad. They almost cost me my business.

Allan: So I guess it boils down to the real reason you switched to XYZ & Co. was that the other firm almost cost you your business, not necessarily that their fees were too high? Would you have paid even higher fees just to get the kind of service you needed to make the right decisions at the right time and avoid the problems you had?

Smith: Damn straight.

As mentioned earlier, people buy for emotional reasons and justify their purchases intellectually. As you'll recall, when I asked Mr. Smith initially why he had switched firms, he said that the previous firm's fees were "way out of line." However, the real reason he changed was that, in his eyes, the previous firm "almost cost me my business" (a highly emotional issue, indeed).

The real problem was not fees. That was his intellectual justification, on the surface, for why he switched firms. Mr. Smith's hurt was the pain and suffering he endured because his business was put in jeopardy.

This is why it is vital to hold yourself back and search for the patient's hurt. If this had been a selling situation and my client had responded to Mr. Smith's initial (stated) concern that his CPA firm's fees were too high, they would have made an incorrect diagnosis and offered the wrong solution. If they had sold into high fees, they might have decided to put a more junior staff person on the job with less partner involvement in order to save the prospective client money. That would have been exactly the wrong solution, and they would have lost the sale.

Only by delving deeper, searching for where it hurt, were they able to correctly diagnose why Mr. Smith was replacing his CPAs. And the issue wasn't fees.

Another Example of the Hurt Analogy

Sharon had wanted a Mercedes convertible for years. She even dreamed about how she'd look driving it: She could smell the upholstery and feel the leather seats and the power as she accelerated. Her brother Bob, a successful attorney, had owned several. Every holiday, he'd tease his little sister, dangling his car keys in front of her and asking her when she would be able to afford a car like his.

Sharon's husband, Rich, could never understand her intense desire for an expensive car. He was extremely cost-conscious and utilitarian by nature. He drove a Nissan Sentra because it took him to and from work.

Finally the day came when Sharon was promoted to the partnership of a consulting firm. She had worked diligently for twelve years to get to that point in her career. Her reward? You guessed it. Right after work that day, she marched over to the closest Mercedes dealership and drove out with a present to herself, a new fire-engine-red convertible. Cost? Roughly $80,000.

Emotionally, she had craved this car for years. Even her big-shot brother didn't own the latest model; would he be shocked! Intellectually, she told herself that she had deserved this reward for her tireless efforts to reach this zenith of her professional career.

However, she knew she was in trouble the minute the tires hit the pavement. What would she tell Rich? That she wanted one? To show her brother? An $80,000 reward?

She needed to create a list of intellectual reasons (a.k.a. excuses) for purchasing the Mercedes. Here's the list that she came up with:

- Now that she was a successful partner, she would have to look the part to her clients and referral sources. [Pretty good, but Rich was also a partner at his firm and he drove an $11,000 car. She needed more.]
- She deserved it as her reward for hard work. [Also pretty good,

except that they didn't celebrate Rich's promotion at all because he didn't want to waste the money at a fancy restaurant.]
- She needed a car that was totally reliable. As a woman, she feared being stranded in the wrong neighborhood. [That was better; her safety was a concern of Rich's. However, wouldn't a reliable car at one-sixth the cost do equally as well?]
- Mercedes automobiles do not depreciate in value that much, and, depending on the movement of the dollar, might even appreciate in value. [But that excuse was weak because Rich managed their investments and the conversation would turn to opportunity costs of money not now being invested because it had been spent on a car.]
- The car was built like a miniature tank—much sturdier than a Japanese sedan. [More safety.]

That was all she could come up with. Rich was not pleased, to say the least. However, she strongly believes the Mercedes purchase went better with Rich than if she had simply told him she had wanted it desperately. Her excuses did lower the negative impact (especially the safety excuses). The one that put Rich over the top was "Would you rather I get crushed to death in another car?"

People buy for emotional reasons (hurts) and then justify their purchases intellectually. In this example, Sharon's hurts included her brother's flaunted success and her positive pain of really wanting a luxurious car to commemorate her promotion. These were the *real* reasons she bought the Mercedes. However, Sharon knew her husband wasn't going to be satisfied with these explanations. Therefore, she created intellectual justifications for buying the car. To him, these justifications were much more acceptable than "Bob has one!" or "I really wanted it!"

In order to sell more effectively, you must understand that this is how people buy. They buy for emotional reasons, then justify their purchases intellectually.

How to Test for Emotional Needs, Wants, Desires, or Musts

There are two distinct parts to Step 2 which need to be conducted in sequence: eliciting information and finding out where it hurts.

Part I: Eliciting Information

In Chapter 7, I mentioned that the best way to establish good personal chemistry is to listen intently. Unless you are naturally gifted at the art of small talk, asking informational questions is the perfect way to commence a sales interview. Also, starting with informational questions allows you to be in control of the conversation, making it more likely that the conference will be productive.

The object of this part of Step 2 is to find out all the relevant information you need to assess correctly the situation for the probability of a sale. Also, asking for information is nonthreatening and starts the prospective client talking.

Preparation for the Interview

Don't make the most common blunder in this step: Never trust to memory or luck the informational questions that you will ask the prospective client in your sales interview.

Recently I had the opportunity to review course materials from a program taught on the West Coast. This program was supposed to teach consultants how to sell. In the materials, the instructor indicated that it was vital to have two questions prepared for the sales interview before going into the presentation of how you can help the buyer.

Excuse me—two questions? That'll take about two minutes or less of the interview because you start spilling your guts about how great you and your firm are, and thus totally lose control of the sale and the likelihood of making that sale! No wonder things are so tough out there—people are taking this man's course and nobody's selling anything to anybody!

No! No! No! You need to have a minimum of twenty informational questions prepared ahead of time; you could have as many as forty. These questions are vital: They enable you to dig up all the information you need to determine if the buyer is qualified to purchase, and, most important, to take total control of the sale and get them talking continuously. Ninety-nine percent of all the buyers I've ever run into loved the sound of their own voice more than mine.

And, yes, you will need to have prepared the hurt-generating questions I will teach you later on in this chapter. In about three years, you may want to take the chance of not having written questions prepared. Until then, why risk the loss of the sale?

A student in one of my courses asked, "What will the buyer

think if he sees you reading questions off a sheet of paper during the sales interview?" My experience is that the buyer will think you are well-prepared, unlike the majority of fools who try to sell him stuff every day, who haven't taken the time to write questions down.

Controlling the Interview

As with a physician conducting a physical examination, you must be in control of the sales process (the sales examination). It is vital to take command of the interview from the get-go. Sometimes people will hit you right off the bat with the "What are your fees?" question. Just like a doctor, you must not discuss fees before you diagnose your patient. How can you tell someone how much it costs before you've had a chance to examine them?

Begin the interview by asking the buyer for a little background information concerning the situation that you are meeting about. Ask "who, what, when, where, why, and how" questions to keep the conversation going. If the prospect does ask about your fees, here's your defense against that deadly line of questioning: "Stella, I'll be happy to answer all of your questions. I just would like to get some background information first."

Afraid to ask questions? Only five people in the last fourteen years—out of more than 1,500 interviews—have refused to answer my questions. This step makes a great deal of sense to the serious prospective buyer because they also want the best solutions to their problems.

A great way to get people talking, to create the right feelings for you, and to have them eventually tell you exactly how to sell them is to create a question that you feel they are absolutely dying to answer. In order to invent this golden question, ask yourself the following: "What question would this person really like to answer?" In the example below, note which question the consultant asks the buyer that really creates the mood that will facilitate the sale.

How the Interview Will Sound

A typical informational questioning strategy would sound like this real-life interview I attended with one of my clients:

Consultant: John, I'm so glad you could meet me for lunch. It was nice of Joe Dokes to refer you to me. Did he say anything about our firm, by chance?

Buyer: Not really. He just told me that I should meet with you before I make any final decision on who to give our computer consulting work to. Evidently you work for some of Joe's other clients as well.

Consultant: Yes. I believe we work with eight of Joe's clients. I'd appreciate it if you could give me some background information about you and your company so we can get a better idea of what you do.

Buyer: We were founded by my dad shortly after he returned from World War II in 1947. Dad had been a fastener salesman before the war and wanted to work for himself. He saw a need for a specialty fastener manufacturer. Dad retired in 1973, and I took over.

Consultant: Exactly what kind of fasteners do you make?

Buyer: We primarily make custom nails for roofing and fascia, although we have even made some specialized bolts for the NASA Apollo program. Our screws were on the moon!

Consultant: Really? Congratulations! How did you manage to get that job? [*This is a key question that will separate this consultant from his competition and shift the sale into his corner. It is beyond the scope of a normal sales interview and will put the buyer on the edge of his seat as he answers it. This is a key question for the consultant to ask because he knows the buyer can't wait to answer it.*]

Buyer: We have quite a reputation for quality in the industry. We competed against eighteen other companies over six months of intensive interviews with NASA's purchasing people and testing engineers. Gosh, it was tough to accomplish, but it was well worth it.

Consultant: How many people do you have working for you?

Buyer: We've got thirty-seven people in the plant making the fasteners and seven people in our office including our data processing manager.

Consultant: Any locations besides the one here in Podunk?

Buyer: We did have one in Peoria, but we had to close that one down because so many of our midwestern customers went out of business. Right now we have a new facility in Coral Springs, Florida, for our customers in the Sun Belt.

Consultant: How do you get your business? Is it mostly old, established accounts, or do you constantly have to hunt down new business?

Buyer: A lot of the old mainstay businesses we dealt with have fallen by the wayside. It's been only recently that we've seen much growth, particularly from Japanese automobile manufacturers building cars in the U.S. They're very picky. We can build to their specs much more consistently than some other fastener makers.

You get the idea. People love to talk about their businesses and themselves. They rarely get the opportunity—until you show up and keep your mouth shut.

Many of the consultants, engineers, appraisers, CPAs, attorneys, architects, and other professional service-providers I train tell me they're afraid of making the wrong impression. They feel they must know everything about a prospective client's company before they walk into a sales interview.

While it helps to have an idea of the situation before you walk in (a third party's assessment of the buyer's hurts would be nice), I am dead-set against spending a lot of valuable time researching a company before a sales call. Not only is your time a scarce asset, but if you know everything about a client before you walk in, you'll be much less likely to ask questions at the interview.

Once you get the patient talking about information, you have accomplished the first part of Step 2. However, make sure you don't elicit only information. You can't sell into information because it is intellectual by nature, not emotional.

Part II: Finding Out Where It Hurts

After you have succeeded at getting the prospective client talking, you should proceed to determining the extent (or lack) of the buyer's emotional needs, wants, desires, and musts.

There are several proven methods you can use to find out where it hurts.

The Natural Progression Method

This is the formula I use predominantly. If you are patient, if you keep your mouth shut, and if you've set the meeting up in the right place, you will find that there is a natural progression of conversation from information to where it hurts. If you're listening to the buyer, you should notice the shift from intellectual and factual information to emotion-laden statements.

The buyer's hurts often appear in their stories about their situation: "I'll never forget the time the engineers called looking for our updated blueprints. Our architect had been late with them and then kept only a copy for herself. She was on vacation and nobody could locate them. We had to stop work right in the middle of the project! Turned out that the drawings were sitting right on top of her desk. . . ."

Mark these emotional statements in your notes with a circled "H" (hurt) for future reference. Refer to Exhibit 4, a mock-up of notes from a typical sales call. If you follow this approach, you can watch

Exhibit 4. A professional's notes from a sales interview.

Questions & Issues	Jack Smith ABC Fasteners — 6/30/94 President 305/555-6789

> why meet?
> who are
 current
 consultants?
> how long
 with them?
(H)
> fees paying?
> +/− (H)
> Conditions
of satisfaction
> decision—
 makers? (H)
 (H)
> Pension (H)
plans?
> when (H)
start? (H)
 (H)
 (H)
 (H)
	— referred by Joe Dokes
	— business since 1917
	— he took over in 1973
	— makes nails for roofs, etc.
	— great reputation! — did NASA project
	— 37 employees
	— 2 loc's: Podunk & Coral Springs, FL
	— industry has shrunk
	— doing business with Japanese
	— considering changing consultants
	— Partner on this client retired
	  2 years ago — replaced by
	  junior partner with no
	  experience in industry
	— never even sees junior partner!
	— no ideas; no input — no value
	— wants someone outside to
	  bounce ideas off of
	— tired of feeling second rate as client
	— no proactive planning
	— continued broken promises
	— constant rotation of inexperienced people
	— wastes time training their staff

as your notes progress from information and facts down the page to the prospective client's hurts.

The Plus/Minus Approach

Here's a very useful way for beginners to find the hurts. Utilizing this method, you will test for what's working with the buyers' current consultant or existing state of affairs and what they like about the relationship or the situation. Then you will test for what they don't like and what's not working (their hurts).

Your prospective clients are inundated with salespeople attempting to sell them things. Most, including your competitors, generally ask about problems with the current vendor, product, or service provider—if they bother with a questioning strategy at all before going into their pitch.

Problem-seeking questions asked early in the selling situation are personal and too threatening to the buyer. They should be avoided until you and the prospective client start feeling comfortable.

Too many times I've seen professionals start their questions with, "What problems are you having with your computer system?" And, taken aback at this intimidation, the buyer invariably says, "Problems? Who said anything about problems?"

The plus/minus approach is much more effective, applied after you have asked the patient some nonthreatening informational questions to get them talking. Also, the prospective client doesn't expect competing service providers to ask what he likes about the current situation.

The plus/minus approach is also a good approach because it bleeds out those people you shouldn't waste time with. If they are overly positive about their current service provider or situation, why would they want to switch? They might simply be on a fishing expedition for free advice.

Continuing from the information-gathering part of the conversation with a prospective client:

Consultant: John, what would you like to accomplish in our conversation today?
Buyer: I'd like to find out about your firm and how you might help me with my business.
Consultant: Who are you using now for your computer consulting?
Buyer: We're using Black, White, and Green.

Consultant: What do you like about working with them? That information would help me get a better handle on how we might help.

Buyer: Not much. Oh, they've given us good work through the years, I guess. But Jack Black, who used to handle our account, retired two years ago, and they gave us one of their junior people. We never see this guy at all. Jack used to sit down with me on a regular basis and discuss what was going on in the business. He's the guy that came up with installing a just-in-time computerized inventory control system and then pursued Japanese car makers as customers. I've kept the old firm out of respect for Jack. But this new guy doesn't give me any input at all. Worse, he speaks in Fortran, not English. I need someone to bounce ideas off of. They sic me with their junior staff and my DP Manager spends her time training their people!

Consultant: When you discussed this situation with them, what did they say?

Buyer: Oh, they've made lots of promises, but little has changed. I feel like a second-rate client.

Bingo! Using this approach, we've started to find out where it hurts. We didn't even get a chance to ask about what wasn't working in the relationship. As happens quite often with a serious buyer, he couldn't wait to tell us his hurts, as long as we kept our mouths shut and didn't interrupt him.

Let's look at the other side. If, for instance, the buyer had responded that he was pleased with his current consultant and that there were no burning issues to talk about as to what wasn't working, we would have a patient in front of us who was fine. Although we could proceed further in looking for where it hurts, chances are this buyer is just "browsing" and isn't really a buyer at all. Since you are in control of the sales interview, you might choose to terminate the conversation politely at that point, rather than waste your time.

Nobody's Perfect

Got a tight-lipped buyer in front of you? Hearing a lot of yes/no answers? Try this approach to open her up:

Consultant: Sally, nobody's perfect. If there was one thing you would change about your current attorney, what would it be?

Buyer: Well, I haven't been pleased with the person they have doing the research work on our litigation this year. In the past, we dealt with Jenny, but she got pregnant and isn't coming back to work. Their new guy hasn't said a word since he started, and his bills, which aren't broken out in any way, are much highier than hers were. Whenever he is here, he spends a lot of time using our phone for personal matters, and he always talks down to me.

The reason that this method works nicely is that everyone knows that nobody, or nothing, is perfect. Warning! If you still don't feel any hurt coming from the buyer, you probably don't have a serious prospective client in front of you.

Another reason this approach is good is that you can use it to discover hurt about any situation. Use it with your current clients to find out about additional services they might need. That might sound like this:

Consultant: Nothing's perfect, Bob. If there was one thing you could change about your payroll system, what would it be?
Client: I wish we could get our computer to process our payroll in less than four passes.
Consultant: What effect is that having on your DP department?
Client: I tell you, these people are putting in all sorts of crazy over-time, and it's costing me a fortune.

Aha! It hurts in the computer department. Can you prescribe a solution, doctor?

Take Them into the Ozone

All too often, conversations with prospective clients and current clients about new work center on fees. If only we could find out what they would really like to have done for once, without regard to fees, then we could do the job that should be done!

Now you have it. The following question and ensuing interaction is designed to take the buyer into the outer limits, into the rhetorical, and away from fees. This way we can find out what all of their hurts are and have them begin to eliminate fee objections for themselves. That's the ideal sale, when the client sells herself.

Consultant: Jane, what role would you want your marketing consul-tant to play if fees really weren't an issue?
Jane: I hadn't really thought about that. We're just looking for a new

set of brochures. Gee, if fees weren't an issue, I could really use some outside input on my advertising on a regular basis.

Consultant: Aren't you getting that now?

Jane: I'm afraid not. Every time we sneeze, our advertising agency charges us for saying "Gesundheit"! Our rep even has the nerve to charge me for his time when he invites me out to lunch. I don't like being taken advantage of, so I have as little contact with him as possible. Please don't get me wrong; I'm not looking for free work. I just need to not be afraid that every time we have contact, you're going to charge me by the minute.

Consultant: How would this additional feedback and contact help you in running your business better?

Jane: Needless to say, I'm not an marketing expert. People in your business have the ability to give us outside feedback for important advertising decisions we face. You see a lot of other businesses and are in the marketplace a lot. We need that kind of input from someone that isn't emotionally involved with our business.

Consultant: Are there any other areas where we might be of service?

Jane: We need someone to take a look at our cold-calling program. . . .

By taking the buyer's concentration away from fees, we have freed her up to discuss her pressing business problems, needs, wants, and desires. The more she talks, the more she will realize that she needs our help. And, since we aren't interrupting her with our mindless banter, she has found someone who obviously cares about her and her business. Why should she hire anyone else?

The Tell Them Where It Should Hurt Method

At times you might not be able to think of a question to keep the conversation moving, or the prospective client may be answering in monosyllabic grunts. That's a good opportunity to inform the buyer about where it should hurt, and then test to see if it does, indeed, hurt there. This is akin to having a physician poke you in places around the abdomen looking for a bad appendix.

Consultant: Phil, often when I meet with prospective clients, I hear the same concerns expressed over and over again about their existing situation. Usually I hear things like their consultant isn't responsive, or they never see the person they hired, or there are mistakes being made repeatedly despite conversations with the person in charge of the account. Often, they complain that there really isn't much communication outside of the time the consultants appear to do the actual work.

Do any of these concerns hit home with you? Is your situation similar?

Phil: Oh yes. Our current firm has made one mistake too many this time. Don't be mistaken; we don't like shuttling between service providers. It's so time-consuming! But this time we were embarrassed before our board of directors because the strategic plans weren't on time for the board meeting. It made us look very bad. . . ."

If the buyer were to respond with "Not really," without taking the bait to open up, you would be meeting with a non-buyer. In that case, you could say:

Consultant: Well, then what are the areas of concern with your existing circumstances that we should discuss?

If that doesn't help the prospective client access his emotional wants, needs, desires, and musts, you can now decide to leave or continue on with a likely shopper (not a buyer). You are in control.

"Are Fees Your Only Consideration . . . ?"

I always suggest that professional service providers not be afraid to approach the tender subject of fees, for many reasons that we will discuss in the next chapter. Addressing the fee issue in this step is valuable to help you avoid price shoppers and to find out what the buyer's hurts are.

Consultant: Lou, I'd like to find out early what your concerns are about hiring the right health benefits firm. Are fees your most important consideration in making the decision whom to go with?

Lou: Absolutely! We see no reason to pay any more than we have to.

Now what? You are in control. You can decide to buy the business by being lowest bidder. If you don't like competing on price, you could still continue, probing for the buyer's other concerns; after all, what have you got to lose? You might proceed:

Consultant: Let's get this straight. All you're interested in is the lowest possible price. Timeliness, quality of work, input as to how to perhaps better run this area of your business, dealing with a firm that your insurance carriers respect, those aren't concerns of yours, right?

You might hear in response:

Lou: I never said that. . . .
Consultant: Then what are your major concerns and why?
Lou: Of course, all of the things you mentioned are important to us. Every firm we've ever dealt with has been no more than glorified and expensive clerks. We've never received any worthwhile help from any of them. If we could be assured that we would receive "X" . . . , then fees wouldn't be the most important issue.
Consultant: How can we help you then?

Or you might hear:

Lou: I never said that, but fees are the predominant issue. All health benefit firms are the same. . . .

You can now decide if you want to compete on price in that situation, or you can leave. You're in control.

Conditions of Satisfaction

As you know, managing client relationships from the very beginning is highly important to keeping clients. Here is the other method (beside the Natural Progression approach) that I use. This method is effective at finding out where it hurts and discovering what it will take to have a very satisfied client.

Also, using this method, we can detect beforehand whether the client's expectations are reasonable and can be fulfilled. It is better to manage expectations before, rather than after, the client is disappointed.

This subject can be approached anytime after the buyers are comfortable with you and have been answering your informational questions for a while:

Consultant: When I bring new clients into the firm, I like to find out very early on what it is going to take to satisfy them. I call these client expectations "Conditions of Satisfaction."

Although you may have not thoroughly considered this subject, what evidence will you need to see six months down the road to determine whether you have made the right decision if you decide to hire us?

Buyer 1: You're right! We haven't given this subject a lot of discussion or thought, perhaps because no other person has ever asked how we'd be satisfied after they started working with us.

For me personally, as controller I would be satisfied by seeing as little interference with our daily work as possible. The last two CPAs we've used have looked upon their audit as the most important event in the world. They've disrupted me and my staff constantly. I think there must be a better way to accumulate information and conduct an audit than barging into my office anytime someone had a whim.

Buyer 2: As CFO, I'm not involved in the day-to-day accounting work or the annual audit. I could use much more advice in the areas of our benefit plans and taxation. I'd be happy if we could finally get our inventory under control and improve our cash position.

Buyer 3: I'm not an accountant and don't really understand—nor care to—the daily goings-on in that area. As president, I must be focused on how to bring in more business, how to motivate our sales management team and salespeople. The best way to make me content is to keep those two out of my hair regarding problems with their audit.

Consultant: So, if we could accomplish those items, you would be satisfied?

Buyer 1: Yes.

Buyer 2: Absolutely.

Buyer 3: Yes.

Consultant: Is there anything else that we've missed?

Buyer 2: Yes, now that I've had a chance to think about it, would you. . . .

Let's step back for a moment and find out what we have accomplished by asking just one question:

1. We have found out where it hurts for all of the buyers. Note that they each had different hurts.
2. We've planted the idea for a future meeting after being hired to discuss how the client relationship is going. This would be a superb time to elicit a referral or two, if the client is satisfied and we have managed the project appropriately.

3. We have separated ourselves from the competition. I promise you that nobody has asked your prospective clients this question before. Ninety-nine percent of all professional service providers and salespeople out there are much more anxious to tell the buyer how great they and their companies are.
4. They have already started using our services, subconsciously! By asking this question, we have placed the prospective clients in the psychological position of having used our services for six months. They have passed that point of fear of decision and we're already working with them!
5. Conditions of Satisfaction can be elicited in any situation, discussing any possible sale of service.

Diagnosing the Patient

Now let's diagnose this situation as to the probability of a completed sale. If the buyers have told you what it will take to be satisfied, if you clear fees (Chapter 8), if there is good chemistry between you, and if you can find out exactly what the decision-making process is and make sure that you are in front of people who can make a decision, why wouldn't they buy you? They'd have to be neurotic.

You need to stop looking at buyers through the eyes of a professional service provider and consider that prospective clients may well be in a position to buy without researching every firm in the Western Hemisphere.

Much more often than not, CEOs and other businesspeople are results-oriented and tend to have great influence over their subordinates. In many instances, buyers find the process of hiring a consultant very tedious and time-consuming; it takes them away from more important duties like increasing sales and keeping the customers happy. When you get to deal with final decision-makers in a selling situation, you must be prepared to walk out of their office with the business. You must be mentally equipped to enroll a new client every time you meet with one.

And Now, A Word about Money

In my illustrations, I have concentrated mostly on circumstances where fees were not the primary issue. Of course, we both know that fees are often a major concern, even if they're not the buyer's primary interest.

My goal is to have you realize that fee problems are most often a symptom of some other hurt and not the real problem. However, money is a painful subject in today's economy. You should remember that by using this doctor's approach to systematic selling you are in control. You can decide where to compete on price. You can also delve deeper to find out what the real problems, needs, wants, desires, and musts are, and take the conversation away from fees.

You will certainly find that the more hurts, needs, wants, desires, and musts there are, the more willing the buyer will be to pay fees. How much would you pay to save your child's life?

This physician's approach does not look for hot buttons, which are on the surface and often easy to solve. You must look much deeper, and listen much more thoroughly, before tossing out solutions to problems and desires. That's why you aren't ready to do a presentation at this point. More qualification is necessary.

Step 3: Test for Commitment to Action

After you have succeeded at finding out where it hurts, you must progress to determining the extent (or lack) of the buyer's commitment to be healed.

The purpose of Step 3 is to separate complainers from action-takers and to avoid wasting time and effort in situations that only result in leaving a bad taste in your mouth.

Selling Rule: People can have all the pain in the world, but unless they are committed to doing something about it, nothing will happen.

There are a couple of ways we can test to see if the prospective client has commitment:

A. Listen for signs of commitment like starting dates:

Buyer: We're going to have this in motion by the thirty-first in order to meet the deadline with the board of directors.

B. Ask for commitment.

Consultant: Jane, thank you for sharing your concerns with me. Sometimes I come in contact with people who have issues that need to be dealt with, but, for whatever reason, they procrastinate and the situation tends to get worse. Are you folks serious about taking care of this right away? Do you have any target dates or a deadline?

Jane: Oh yes. We can't let this go on much longer.

As mentioned previously, you must be prepared to be hired at any time. You will find, as I and many of the best business developers in the professions have, that you may be hired at the completion of this step.

Do not offer to do a proposal! You must be comfortable with securing the client now, if you want them. Sometimes, there is so much hurt and the chemistry is so good, that the client will decide to engage you immediately. Don't talk yourself out of a sale!

Let's recap Steps 2 and 3 and decide whether to proceed in the sales interview. In these important steps, you have done all that you can to have the prospective client share with you their emotional needs, wants, and desires, and you have tested for commitment. Asking questions and listening without interruption have also boosted the personal chemistry with the buyer.

Now you need to determine how, and if, to proceed. Test the amount and nature of the hurts you have listened to. Was the prospective client emotionally involved? Did they speak openly and freely? Are they committed?

If hurts and commitment are lacking, you can decide to terminate the sale at this point. And why not? Unless you are looking for more practice selling and being used as a free resource for ideas, now is a good time to decide if it's worth the effort to stay involved. Save that precious commodity known as your self-esteem.

Remember: One of the most important words in selling more professional services is "Next?"

If the prospective client has passed Steps 2 and 3, we can now proceed to Step 4: Test for Ability and Desire to Pay.

Diagnosis and Rx: Find Out Where It Hurts

- In order to sell effectively, you need to understand *why people buy*. An important selling rule to remember: People buy for emotional reasons and then justify their purchases intellectually.
- If you make a thorough examination and discover that the buyer

is fine—the buyer has revealed no emotional needs, wants, desires, or musts—a sale cannot be made.

▸ When questioning/examining your prospect, you must dig deep; don't accept what they say at face value. If the buyer states she is changing providers because her current one charges fees that are too high, don't assume that's the real problem. Ask her to tell you about it. Hold yourself back from offering solutions, and search for the buyer's real hurts.

▸ There are two distinct parts to the examination process that must be conducted in sequence; the first one is eliciting information. Ask informational questions to start the conversation. Keep asking them in order to discover all the relevant information you'll need to correctly diagnose the buyer's problem and to assess the situation for the probability of a sale. You should have a minimum of twenty informational questions prepared for each sales call.

▸ Once you get the buyer talking, you should move on to the second part of this step: finding out where it hurts. There are several methods you can use to discover where it hurts: the buyer's emotional needs, wants, desires and musts.

1. *The Natural Progression Method.* Buyers will often drift naturally from providing mere information to telling you more valuable details about their businesses. Listen carefully to their answers and stories, and take special note when they make emotion-laden statements.

2. *The Plus/Minus Approach.* Start by asking your prospective clients what they like about their current supplier, and then patiently work your way to what they don't like (often you won't have to ask; the buyers will get around to telling you eventually, if you keep your mouth shut).

3. *Nobody's Perfect.* When you've got a tight-lipped buyer in front of you, try this approach to open him up: "Fred, nobody's perfect. If there was one thing you could change about your current designer, what would it be?"

4. *Take Them into the Ozone.* If you're having trouble steering the conversation away from the fee issue, you might say, "Jane, what role would you want your accountant to play if fees really weren't an issue?"

5. *The Tell Them Where It Should Hurt Method.* If you are having difficulty thinking of a question, or the prospective client is answering in monosyllabic grunts, it's a good opportunity to in-

form the buyer about where it should hurt, and then test to see if it does, indeed, hurt there. (This is similar to having a physician poke you in places around the abdomen looking for a bad appendix.)

6. *"Are Fees Your Only Consideration?"* Never be afraid to discuss fees. If the prospect is truly buying on price alone, you should be aware of that; then you can decide if you want to compete on price or leave. Also, remember: the deeper the hurt, the more willing the buyer will be to pay; delve deep to find out the real problems.

7. *Conditions of Satisfaction.* You should find out what the buyer's expectations are in order to determine if they are realistic and if you can—or want to—satisfy them.

▸ After you have succeeded in finding out where it hurts, you must progress to determining the extent (or lack) of the buyer's commitment to be healed. There are two ways to do this:

1. Listen for signs of commitment, like starting dates.
2. If none are obvious, ask the buyer if he's serious about taking care of the situation right away, if he has a date planned for implementation, or some such question.

▸ By going through this examination procedure, you have found out where the buyer hurts, you've planted the seed for a good working relationship, and you've separated yourself from the competition. If the buyer does indeed hurt *and* has a desire to do something about it, you're well on your way to making the sale.

8

Conducting a Financial Diagnostic and Nurturing The Desire to Pay

In this chapter, you'll learn how to determine if prospective clients are willing to pay your fees—before you get too far along in the sales process. This is important because the longer you wait to discuss fees, the more emotionally involved you become, which increases the odds that you will cut fees to close the sale.

Why Step 4: Test for Ability and Desire to Pay Is Important

Assuming your patient does have hurts, and that she is committed to having them cured, you now need to find out if she has the ability and willingness to pay to be healed. This is akin to the doctor who checks to see if the patient has insurance coverage before he starts operating.

Of course, fees are a big issue today because of the economy and the increasingly competitive nature of the professions. Some competitors seem to be giving their services away because they are desperate just to generate cash flow. However, using the sales examination to its fullest advantage, you are in control. You decide if you want to compete on price. The sales examination is composed to help the buyer feel where it hurts and see you as the savior—and thus be willing to pay more for your services.

Physicians know that the best time to discuss payment is before the operation or cure. People who are cured have less motivation to pay your fees. Yet many professional service providers cure the prospective patient during the sales interview for free. Then they wonder why they can't close the sale, or why the patient decided to stay with his current provider or do it in-house (using the prospective new provider's ideas, of course).

Here are the reasons for determining ability and willingness to pay early on in the sales process:

1. *Avoid wasting time.* Your time to market and sell is limited and therefore highly valuable. Don't invest this asset with people who have a low probability of paying the fees you need to produce quality work.

2. *Eliminate fee objections early in the selling process.* Very often professional service providers wait too long in the sales interview to discuss fees. They waste time with people who weren't qualified buyers in the first place or wind up cutting their price when they needn't have if the sale had been conducted correctly.

3. *Use emotional momentum to your advantage.* Picture a child on a swing. There are basically three positions that the child can be in on a swing: "up" (positive), neutral (at rest), or "down" (negative). These positions apply also to your prospective clients in the selling situation; they are on an emotional swing and can be positive, neutral, or negative at various points in the process.

Most of the time professionals wait until the end of a sales call to discuss fees, or they avoid the topic altogether. Ninety-nine percent of all proposals have fees listed on the last page.

Outdated selling techniques have taught you to wait until the end of the sale to talk price, because the customer will be so excited that he will gladly pay what you want. Today's sophisticated buyer knows that game all too well.

Using the child's swing as an analogy, you can see that if the buyer is up, he has only one way to go, and vice versa; a body in motion tends to stay in motion. Therefore, a positive buyer is in a dangerous position for you, because he can only go negative.

Too often, many of us have lost the sale at the end of the conversation or later, when the buyer swung back to neutral or negative. In those situations where the buyer has become less positive, it is very difficult to move him back up.

By discussing fees in the middle of the conversation, you can use the emotional swing to your advantage.

An Example of the Swing Analogy

Most of us have had the usually unpleasant experience of buying an automobile. That intense desire to have a new car is similar to the feeling of wanting a new toy when we were children. We are positive on the emotional swing.

So, you trudge into the dealership, wary of any sales-types who stand ready to pounce on you. You look around. Aha! There it is: the new Eliminator, the car of your dreams! Slowly, in awe, you stroll over to it. You know what awaits: the outrageous price. As you gaze upon the price sticker, you swing wildly negative. It's even worse than you thought it would be! These dealers are insane! You are now negative on the emotional swing.

A very smart salesperson approaches delicately. She doesn't want to scare you off. She asks softly if you have driven the new model of the Eliminator and hands you the keys for a test spin by yourself.

As you enter the car, you alight on the soft leather seats. Oh, they feel so good! You turn the key and hear the purr of the engine. In anticipation, like a child unwrapping a new toy on Christmas morn, you speedily drive off the lot and into the street. VRRROOOMMM!!!!

You accelerate quickly. The car is so powerful, so strong, so safe. You start selling the new car to yourself: "I deserve this car. I work so very hard, I need some pleasure in my life. . . . I'll be much safer in this car—no more worry about getting to my clients. . . . I can afford an extra couple of thousand dollars for this. Ooooohhhhh."

As you pull back into the dearlership, you have returned to positive on the emotional swing. The salesperson awaits. Because she has learned her lessons well, she knows not to turn this situation into a negotiating war. She wants to remove your defenses to facilitate the sale and keep you positive.

You walk in, and she directs you into a room and makes you feel like a guest in her home. She offers coffee and, realizing you are in a dangerous position on the emotional swing, closes the deal as quickly and gingerly as possible. You drive home happy with your new toy.

In this example, you can see several powerful selling strategies at work. You, the customer, are allowed to sell yourself. There was terrific emotional involvement by the time you were forced into the unpleasant experience of negotiating price with a car dealer. The salesperson was smart enough to know that she had to keep you positive by allaying your defense systems and closing the deal as quickly as possible.

Please understand that, because the way this selling situation was set up by the intelligent, experienced, and successful salesperson, you were virtually magnetized to the positive sector of the emotional swing. You sold yourself before sitting down to battle over price. The swing had gone so far positive that the deal would still be made to the benefit of both.

How the Swing Affects Professional Service Providers

Prospective clients are much more likely to pay higher fees if they are emotionally involved in the sales process. The swing can become magnetized if you start to discuss fees at the right time, and clients will be more likely to pay higher fees than they would have otherwise. Also, there is still time for the swing to come back to positive, if fees are parlayed early, rather than as the last issue in the interview or avoided altogether.

Of course, you cannot often give the prospective client a solid fee estimate without further discussion, examination, and analysis of time involved in a project. But, just like the sticker on an automobile, you can give them the opportunity to start selling themselves long before the sales interview is over.

The Wrong Way to Sell

Usually, the customer never gets the opportunity to sell himself in a situation like the car-buying example above. Automobile salespeople are notoriously impatient and try to battle over price before the customer is sufficiently emotionally involved. End result? They wind up losing the sale that should have been made. The customer's emotional swing never gets to the extreme positive, the customer swings too far negatively for the deal to be made, or the customer leaves the dealership to shop around until he finds a car he likes at the absolutely lowest, rock-bottom price.

An Important Lesson

Shopping for the lowest possible price is how you buy cars, right? I bet you probably can't imagine anyone buying a car right off the showroom floor without haggling for days over price.

One of the significant selling lessons I have learned from the best business generators in the professions is to stop and realize that you are probably looking at the world through the eyes of a professional service provider. Be careful! Those of us in the professions tend to be highly intellectual, very analytical, and not as in touch with our emotions as most of our prospective clients are.

Many of the people we sell professional services to are not accountants, consultants, engineers, or any other professional service providers. There are many different personality types (which we will review in Chapter 9), and each should be sold to differently. Many of the clients we sell to are leaders, Norman Schwarzkopf types who are interested in one thing: results. They are not interested in details, and if properly sold, price is secondary. In this step, use the emotional swing to your advantage by discussing fees early, after the client is emotionally involved.

Let the Prospective Client See The Behavior of Someone Who Is Very Successful

People like to do business with people who are successful. If the professional is recognized by the prospective client as being a success in her field, the client is likely to sell himself by coming to the conclusion that the reason the professional is so successful is that she is very good at what she does.

Much of what we do and how we act represents us better than what we say. The words we say are a very small part of our total communication. The science of neuro-linguistic programming (NLP) reveals that only approximately 7 percent of our communication is through the words we speak. Thirty-eight percent of our communication is through the tones in which we speak, and a full 55 percent of our communication is through how we act, how we come across, to others.

This is an important selling lesson to learn; it explains one reason why Ronald Reagan was so successful as president. Not too many people can remember much of what Mr. Reagan said when he was president. However, didn't he look like a president? Didn't the words he spoke sound great? He didn't carry his own suit bag onto Air Force One as Jimmy Carter did. The president is the most powerful person in the world; he should look and act the part!

Buyers are afraid to deal with people who need the business. Highly successful professionals who bring in a lot of business to their firm do not waste a lot of time dillydallying around fees. They are confident in their abilities and expect clients to pay for their valuable services. They realize their own value and are sold themselves on their fees. By discussing fees relatively early in the sales process, you are giving the prospective client the behavior of someone very successful.

Keep Control of the Selling Process

Ah, control; that is a very important word to a professional service provider. Many professionals have a passion to control everything. Every *i* must be dotted, every *t* crossed. Where's the to-do list? We must not let the project get out of control!

And so it is with the sales process. You must be in control of this delicate procedure, or accidents may happen which can cause you to fail. You must discuss fees after discovering the client's hurts because it keeps you in control, enabling you to guarantee the best possible outcome.

The Transition from Step 3 to Step 4

Let's review where you are in the sales interview:

- You and the prospective client have been developing a comfortability and chemistry with each other.
- The client is telling you his emotional needs, wants, desires, and musts, as well as the background information necessary for you to diagnose the situation.
- The buyer is committed to action.

Now, we need a transition to discuss fees:

Consultant: Bob, thanks for discussing these issues with me. I believe I have a good perspective on your situation. Usually, I find that now is a good time to discuss our fees. I don't want to waste your time. Is that okay with you?
Buyer: Sure.

In fourteen years of approaching buyers at this time about fees (after listening to where it hurts for forty-five minutes to an hour or so), no prospective client has ever said that it was too early to discuss fees. It just makes too much sense; in this way, you're not leading people on. Usually, I've found that we professionals are the ones who are afraid to approach the subject.

How to Perform Step 4

Here are five ways to approach the subject of fees. Select one or two that you feel comfortable with:

1. *Ask for a budget.*

Professional: Do you have a budget for this project/engagement?

Sometimes people will share their budget with you; other times, they won't. I've found this depends on the level of chemistry (and ensuing trust) between you and the prospective client. Buyers usually have a budget, especially if you are discussing a project.

Some people will say to you "as little as possible." That's okay. Option 2 is a good way to follow up that remark.

2. *Ask, "Are fees your most important consideration?"* Smoke 'em out early, I say. You should maintain control and decide whether you want to buy the work and deal with people who are only interested in fees.

Consultant: Betsy, are fees your most important consideration in hiring a new consultant (or completing this systems project)?
Betsy: Yes. We want the cheapest we can find.

You're in control in Step 4, and now you know what you're dealing with. This is before you've become emotionally involved, spent a great deal of time, or done a lot of work on a proposal or a presentation. You can decide if and how to proceed:

Usually, however, the dialogue will go like this:

Consultant: Betsy, are fees your most important consideration in hiring a new consultant?
Betsy: No. Of course, fees are a consideration, but we're very concerned about getting this project done on time and getting our building finished. The longer it takes to complete, the more we lose on rent and credibility to our investors and future tenants. And we want the easiest transition from our old architects, with the least disruption of staff.

Good. Hopefully you have flushed out the fee issue. You have discovered some additional information (or if you've done your job correctly in Step 2, a verification of where it hurts). My experience, and that of my clients, is that Betsy is likely to pay more for the right person who she perceives will perform valiantly to solve her hurts.

3. *Throw a ballpark figure at them.* This is my favorite method to discuss fees.

> *CPA:* Jonathan, based on what we've discussed so far, you're looking at a range of $8,000 to $12,000 for our fees. That estimate could be somewhat high or low. Unfortunately, I can't be more precise at this time because I haven't inspected your books and records and calculated the hours needed to complete the project. But that's a good ballpark figure. Should we continue talking?

You have just closed the buyer for fees. If he says yes, you should go forward, because he has passed Step 4. If he says no, he has failed to qualify for fees. You could then find our what he wanted to pay and decide whether you desire the business at that price, or whether you should simply thank him for his time and leave.

Some professional service providers say they do not like using a ballpark figure. After all, they need to calculate, recalculate, analyze, discuss, think about, mull over, and contemplate what the engagement entails. Ah, baloney! Give the buyer a ballpark figure and don't waste your time. You need to move on with the sales interview. Now's the best time to get the fee issue under control.

4. *Ask the buyer, "What are you paying now?"*

> *Professional:* Stacy, what kind of fees are you paying your current firm?

If the buyer won't answer this question, be on alert. She should feel comfortable by now and trust you. If she isn't willing to tell you, she is playing games because she is afraid of being taken advantage of. At this point, it is a danger signal if the buyer refuses to tell you what she is paying.

5. *Tell the buyer, "We're rarely cheapest and might be more expensive. Should we continue?"*

> *Professional:* Chris, thank you for discussing your situation with me. Usually, I find that this is a good time to discuss fees, as I don't like leading people on.

In most circumstances like yours, we're rarely cheapest and might be more expensive—should we continue?
Chris: Okay.

Again, if you discover that the buyer is only interested in fees, you are still in control and can decide if and how to proceed.

Buying the Business

The purpose of the sales examination is to put you in total control of the selling process, just the way a physician is in control of the examination process. By being in control, you can decide with whom, and how, you want to do business.

Unfortunately, the only way many professionals know how to sell is by cutting fees. I've met some service providers who are so bad at selling that they literally couldn't give it away; that's right—they couldn't get the prospective client to take it for free.

And, fortunately for you, less than 5 percent of your competition would even consider reading a book like this. The professional service provider who knows how to sell can realize their dreams of financial success and freedom. You have much less competition than you might think.

There are going to be times, however, when you may want to consider buying the business in order to open a new market or get a specific client. It has to be your decision. Just don't make it a matter of habit in your selling.

The very first large consulting client I procured way back when was sold on the condition that I work for half of my normal fee. I took that offer—with the up-front contract that they would act as a referral source. I did that because I knew that having a client like them in a position to give me referrals and be a shining point for future prospective clients to see would be well worth it. That one major client jump-started my career to the national level, and I worked with them for several years. Even though I cut fees, I will always be grateful for that opportunity.

Many of the smartest professional firms buy market share and exposure in this way—just make sure it is your decision to do so with the understanding up-front that the client will act as a referral source in the future.

How to Proceed in the Sales Interview

In Step 4, you have tested the patient for willingness to pay to have his hurts cured. Now you need to determine how and if to proceed. Are you comfortable with how the prospect views fees? Is he a serious buyer or merely a browser? Is this sales interview and prospective client worthy of pursuit?

If the buyers passed Step 4, we now proceed to Step 5: Knowledge of the Decision-Making Process and the Ability to Influence that Process.

Diagnosis and Rx: Don't Operate Without Insurance

- ► Assuming that your prospective client has pain and is committed to healing, you must also ascertain that she has the ability and willingness to pay for a cure.
- ► The best time to discuss fees is before you've offered any solutions; people who are cured have less motivation to agree to pay your fees. Discuss fees early in order to:

  1. Avoid wasting time. Don't spend your precious sales time with someone who is unwilling or unable to pay your fees.
  2. Eliminate fee objections early in the selling process. This will help you to avoid unqualified buyers and the need to slice fees.
  3. Use emotional momentum to your advantage. If the prospect has an objection to the fees, you're still early enough in the sale to discuss the problem, alleviate the objection, and keep going.

- ► You will find that prospects are much more likely to pay higher fees if they are emotionally involved in the sales process. Be sure that you have reached the real issues that concern your prospect during your sales examination.
- ► Although we professional service-providers tend to be very selective and price-conscious, most of the businesspeople we sell to are not.
- ► Successful professionals do not waste a lot of time quibbling about fees; they are confident in their abilities and expect clients to pay for their valuable services. Act like you are successful, and you will be perceived as successful.

- After you've established chemistry, found hurts and commitment to be healed, you should make the transition to discussing fees; there are five ways to do this:

  1. Ask for a budget.
  2. Ask, "Are fees your most important consideration?"
  3. Throw a ballpark figure at the prospect.
  4. Ask the buyer, "What are you paying now?"
  5. Tell the buyer, "We're rarely cheapest and might be more expensive. Should we continue talking?"

- You should not make a habit of cutting fees to buy the business. However, you may want to make an occasional concession in order to open a new market or acquire a specific client. If you do, make sure that you have an up-front agreement that the client will act as a referral source for you in the future.

9

Anatomy of the Decision-Making Lifeline

In this chapter, you'll learn how to uncover all the viable information about the prospective client's decision-making process. You also discover how to ascertain whether you can influence that process to your benefit. This makes up Step 5: Test for Knowledge of the Decision-Making Process and the Ability to Influence that Process.

Why Testing the Decision-Making Process Is Important

Testing the decision-making process will enable you to:

1. *Ascertain the decision-making process.* In this step you need to find out everything that you possibly can, in order to avoid spending time interviewing the wrong people. As you interview different people, you will find that each has his or her own set of priorities. Selling into the wrong set of objectives is disastrous and will cause you to fail. Also, professional service providers often find out who the true decision-makers are when it's too late, after their presentation or proposal is made.

2. *Avoid wasting time.* Your time to market and sell is limited and valuable. Don't invest this asset with people who have a low probability of making a decision in the near future or are unlikely to decide in your favor. You need to decide if you want to pursue clients who will not let you access the real decision-makers or will not tell you how the decision will be made.

3. *Acquire a mentor who will guide you through the sale to a successful result.* Two heads are better than one, especially in selling. In each sale, you want to find someone who can lead you through the sale

and tell you what it will take to get it. This mentor may be (hopefully) on the inside of the buyer's company, in your own firm, or someone you respect as being highly successful at selling.

4. *Eliminate your competition, if possible.* In this step, you will attempt to eliminate all or most of your competition, in order to put the selling odds in your favor.

5. *Jockey for last position.* A good rule-of-thumb regarding the decision-making process is "He who is last, wins." The last impression is very powerful. We have all lost sales we thought we had won to a less-qualified opponent because we got "lost in the shuffle" when the person who followed us made a more lasting impression.

Different Personality Types That Affect the Decision-Making Process

Not everyone makes decisions in the same way. It will help you to better perform Step 5 if you quickly discern what personality type you are dealing with in the selling situation.

There are six basic personality types you need to be concerned with. You can quickly size people up by observing their behavior, position in the company, and environment.

1. The Leader

Most of the business owners (entrepreneurs) and CEOs of fast-moving, aggressive companies are leaders. Leaders are confident and direct, love challenges, and are willing to take charge and go into action. They are interested foremost in results and like to make things happen. Leaders are goal-oriented, self-motivated, aggressive, and problem-solvers.

These people are action-oriented and dissatisfied with the status quo. Their businesses are a direct extension of them. Many leader clients don't even know how much money they make, year to year. Their motivation for going to work is the thought of playing Monopoly for real. They are not interested in details and are prone to making quick decisions based on their instincts so they can get on to the next battle or issue. They are impatient. If you dillydally about securing a decision, you will lose them because they will have moved on to some other fire to put out.

Norman Schwarzkopf, Mike Ditka, Lee Iacocca, and Margaret

Thatcher are consummate leader personality types. People like them could not care less about the details of what you will do as their service provider. Don't discuss the intricacies of the project; you'll lose them. All they care about is getting the ball over the goal line, ASAP. They want to know how you are going to help them achieve better results and beat their competition.

Leaders like change! They are risk-takers and love speculating. They seek out people committed to winning to be members of their team. If you help them win more often, they will promote you wildly to their friends, other leaders.

The leader's office may be well-appointed, showing off her success. More importantly, it is functional in order to better get things done.

Their hurts and buying motives center around producing better results and beating the competition, which includes personal competitors, such as friends, siblings, and parents; in-house competitors, such as fellow workers; and corporate competitors, like rival companies. They are not generally concerned with issues like how much money they will save on fees.

The one question you must ask a leader is, "How can I, as your consultant (or engineer, attorney, graphic designer, accountant, architect), help you beat the competition?" Ask this of a results-oriented achiever like a leader and you tremendously boost your chemistry, separate yourself from the competition (who hasn't thought of it), and find out how to sell them.

2. The Executive/Manager

Most CEOs, other executives, and managers of established companies fit into this category. They are motivated by what's in it for them personally. Their motivations are looking good to others (the board of directors, their bosses, their employees), their personal security, and their financial compensation. They may not take action if it just benefits the company, if they can't see the connection to how it will help them. Unlike leaders, they do not welcome change or action unless they can see the direct personal benefit.

You must find out how the situation affects them personally and have them tell you how a change or what you are suggesting might help them. Don't forget that fees may not be tantamount to selling these people. Executives/managers spend others' money faster and more easily than they spend their own. A good question to ask an executive/manager is, "How could I, as your consultant, help you to be even more productive and valuable?"

3. The Socializer

Socializers are very amiable and have a wealth of friends. They are people-lovers and are likely to be found in sales and other people-related positions, such as public relations and advertising. They enjoy working with people and hate personal rejection.

Socializers are primarily concerned about their relationships with other people. They covet personal attention from people they deal with. Their office environment may have a real attention-getting item in order to get conversations going. One of my socializer clients has a full-scale model of a pony in his office!

Socializers want to be liked and are uncomfortable with silence. They like to talk—it gives them energy. Their hurts and buying motives tend to center around a lack of personal attention from their professional service provider. Also, they tend to be disorganized and want to put their lives, career, and business in order.

They want more friends, contacts, and customers and are not necessarily interested in results or fees as an issue. You will bore them and lose the sale if you give them unnecessary details. The questions to ask a socializer are, "Does your current service provider give you enough personal attention? Are you as organized as you should be?"

4. The Overseer

Ben Cartwright, a character on the old TV show *Bonanza*, was the perfect overseer: he took care of his family, his people, and the Ponderosa ranch.

Overseers are against change and are selfless. They are motivated by what is best for the "family." Inside organizations, they often are the support people but will also show up as the paternal/maternal figure in the top spot.

They are less interested in bottom-line results and are more concerned with how every move they make affects the organization.

They do not like to rock the boat, and they want their service providers to fit in with the group. Overseers look for cooperation and support of the group's goals. If you are perceived as being too different, you are in trouble. You will bore them and lose the sale if you give them unnecessary details.

Identify overseers by the multitudes of family pictures or their children's drawings in their office. These people are the "hosts" of the world vs. the "guests." Once you get on their side, they'll do anything for you.

Their hurts are the group's hurts. Their buying motives center around the welfare of the company family, not necessarily the bottom line or how much money they'll save on fees. A good question to ask an overseer is, "How could I, as your consultant, help make things better around here for everybody?"

5. The Innovator

You'll find innovators working in arts-related fields, as designers, writers, architects, actors, and musicians. Innovators are not against change; the very nature of what they do is novelty.

Their primary buying motive, or hurt, is to free up time to allow them to create. They are similar to leaders in this way: They will hand you the ball to run with. You will bore them and lose the sale if you provide unnecessary details. Some innovators even turn the management of their business and their financial affairs over to someone else, in order to free up more time for them to create.

Their office or place of business may be quite unusual, messy, and disorganized. These people make decisions quickly. They want to concentrate on innovating. A good question to ask an innovator is, "How could I, as your consultant, free up more quality time for you?"

6. The Accountant/Engineer

Ninety percent of CPAs and engineers possess these personality traits. They are not risk takers but rather are suspicious and very conservative by nature. They follow rules and regulations. They love information and detail. Their offices are organized and tend to be meticulous. Don't touch anything on their desk!

Their buying motives focus on making sure that they get the very best value for themselves and their company, and making their lives easier. Most accountants/engineers believe they work too hard, and they negate change for fear that it will add work to their already busy schedules.

They may change sometime within the next several lifetimes, if they perceive that they are not getting the best deal for their money and that such a change will make their schedules lighter, thus freeing up some time to focus on more important tasks. Don't hold your breath waiting for these people to make a decision.

Accountants/engineers are not open-minded, and they doubt everything. They are against change, are scared to death of failing and taking risks in general, are not interested in anything except bottom-line results, and are primarilay motivated by dying with as much money as possible. Fee issues are paramount.

Their concern with fee issues is one reason accountants/engineers fail so often in the selling situation. As you can see, five out of the six types of decision-makers discussed are not primarily motivated by saving fees. And yet, this is how most accountants/engineers sell; they hope to secure the client by saving fees. By focusing on fees, they totally miss the mark in selling their services.

The way to sell to accountants/engineers is to flood them with information. The more information—details, charts, numbers, case studies—the better, because this multitude of information helps to ease their fear of failure. These people are hot for referrals of people who have hired and used you successfully in the past.

Always follow up thoroughly with accountants/engineers—your goal must be to get past them to the money man or money woman who is the real decision-maker. Accountants/engineers are tough buyers and often postpone decisions that could or should be made.

A couple of good questions to ask an accountant/engineer are, "How could I, as your consultant, help you boost your bottom line?" "How could I provide more value than the person (or company) you are currently using?" "How could we make your life easier around here and open up more time for you?"

Of course, individuals are not one specific type of personality or another. There will be a dominant trait, followed by a secondary quality. For instance, a CEO might be a leader primarily and a socializer secondarily.

What Kind of Decision-Maker Are You?

In selling, what you project out into the world, you will receive in return. If you're the kind of person that has to mull something over for sixteen thousand years before you can finally say yes or no, that is exactly the kind of decision you will receive from prospective buyers and clients. Are people constantly telling you they need more time to "think it over"? No wonder! So do you!

The top business producers in the professions are able to make up their minds quickly. They don't have the time to paralyze the decision-making process and hold back progress. They are comfortable in taking action and don't lose sleep over the few wrong decisions they have made. They know that the longer they wait to do something, the less likely it is that it will happen, so they do it now.

They can walk into a dealership and drive out with a car an hour later. They can also meet with a prospective client and leave with a new client an hour later. Because that is their attitude about making their own decisions, those are the kind of decisions they get: immediate yes's or no's. Anything else would be illogical to them.

Improving Your Hit Ratio

To be more successful at procuring yes or no decisions, practice by going to restaurants. Don't open your menu until the waiter comes, and then decide. Stop saying that you have to think it over in decision-making situations, and start saying yes or no. Do it now! Remember: a decision not to make a decision is still a decision.

To be more successful at selling, quickly identify what type of person you are dealing with, and be more comfortable with having people hire you immediately—even though you might not rush into a decision yourself.

Most successful businesspeople are interested in putting out the immediate fire so they can move on to the next one. Consider dropping all of the unnecessary details of your presentation. And remember, in dealing with other types of decision-makers, fees are often not the dominating issue.

How to Perform Step 5: The Transition from Step 4

Let's review where you are in the sale:

- You and the prospective client have been developing a comfortability and chemistry with each other.
- The client is telling you his emotional needs, wants, and desires, as well as the background information necessary for you to diagnose the situation.
- The buyer is committed to action.
- You are comfortable with the buyer's willingness to pay your fees.

What It Takes to Accomplish Step 5

In this step you need the answer to four questions:

1. *Who* are the decision-makers?
2. *Who* is your competition?
3. *When* will the decision be made?
4. *How* will the decision be made?

An example of Step 5 follows, featuring a professional service provider named Bernie, a CPA, and a prospective client, Bob. Bob is the controller for a manufacturing business with sales of about $7 million.

Although this illustration of selling consulting services relates to the field of accounting, I ask that you try to see how it would work in your own situation. This conversation would not go much differently if Bernie were selling office design, computer consulting, architectural services, or any other professional service.

Over the last fourteen years, I have consulted with every possible type of professional service organization. I promise you that although this situation involves one specific profession, it will not be that much different from your own.

In fact, selling audit services may be more difficult than selling other types of professional services because of the very nature of the marketplace for such services. Over the years, buyers of accounting and audit services have seen these services and the providers in more and more generic terms. Audits are forced on a company by a bank or a government agency and are usually seen as a necessary evil. It is an extremely difficult sale compared to other forms of professional services I am familiar with. There is much less—almost no—perceived value by the client.

I have specifically chosen a most difficult selling situation to show you the value of using this thorough sales examination methodology:

Bernie: Bob, what does the decision-making process look like for this audit?

Bob: We're in the process of interviewing seven CPA firms for this audit. We've invited them all in to discuss their qualifications. After I've conferred with all of them, I'll narrow it down to three firms for Ms. Jones and invite them back to meet with her. Ms. Jones and I will meet then and come to a conclusion about who we will hire.

The Five Decision-Makers Who Affect the Decision-Making Process

It appears Bernie has just answered the questions about who the decision-makers are and how the decision will be made.

But beware! There is frequently—both accidentally and purposely—hidden information you need to learn in order to correctly perform this step. You must always pursue the five types of decision-makers that affect this process:

1. *The money man (or woman).* This person is the final decision-maker and "signs the checks."
2. *The user.* This is the person whom you or your staff interact with. She may be the project manager, office manager, department manager, or something similar. But be careful. This person is most often not the final decision-maker, but she may pass herself off as such. However, she is important because she will have influence with the money man, who will not want to hire someone who won't get along with her.
3. *The outside intruder.* This is the person most often overlooked in the selling process. The outside intruder may be the buyers' valued attorney, banker, accountant, or consultant—the person whom they go to for business advice. You need to get in front of this person if you deem their influence important. Your competition won't think of it.
4. *The intermediate.* Sometimes, you cannot get in front of the final decision-maker. In that instance, you must sell intermediates as if they were that person. In such cases, the final decision-maker is relying on the intermediates for a recommendation on whom to hire. Chances are, the final decision-maker has taken their advice before and will do so again.
5. *Committees.* If a committee is involved in the decision-making process, you should attempt to get in front of them to present your own case. If you cannot, you will have to rely on the intermediate to sell for you (not the best situation).

Let's go back to Bernie's conversation with Bob. Bernie must explore further:

Bernie: So, there is no one else involved in the decision, such as your attorney, for instance?

Bob: Well, Jane Doe is a trusted business advisor to the company and has been our counsel for the last twenty years. We probably wouldn't make a move without her input.

Bernie: Is Ms. Jones the final decision-maker, then?

Bob: We'll be making the decision jointly.

Bernie: Do you think it would be possible for me to get together with Jane Doe? Usually counsel, without divulging confidential information, has a different perspective on the client's business that is quite helpful to us.

Bob: I can't see why she'd mind.

I promise you that Bernie's competition hasn't thought of meeting the company's attorney. Yes, it is possible that the client will say no to such a meeting, but, even in that instance, Bernie will have showed himself to be more thorough than anyone else they will interview (a good quality for every consultant and professional service provider).

And if Bernie does meet with their counsel, he's just made another contact with a potential referral source. Since he would be the only one to meet with her, if he makes a good impression, she will endorse him.

Bernie: May I ask who your banker is?

Bob: It's Nate Rate over at Frank National Bank. Do you know Nate?

Bernie: Why yes, I do. Super guy.

Assuming that Bernie does know Nate, he can contract him (preferably meeting with him for lunch) and ask him to put in a good word. If he doesn't know him, he could ask to meet him.

Now Bernie needs to nail down when the decision will be made and who his competition is:

Bernie: When do you expect to make a decision?

Bob: We want to wrap this up in two weeks.

Bernie: Have you had a chance to meet with any other CPAs yet?

Bob: We've met with one other firm, so far. The rest of the interviews are set up for later this week.

Bernie: May I ask who the other firms are?

Bob: Sure. We've met with Joe Blow and Co., who is our current accountant, and we'll be meeting with Arnold Arneson; Dupers and Hydrant; Young and Olde; Yours, Mine and Ours; and Jack Sprat.

Perhaps you have asked about your competitors before in a sales interview and the buyer has told you that he prefers not to divulge that information. If so, that is a danger signal. Using the sales examination, Bernie has specifically left this particular discussion to later in the interview, in order to give the buyer time to get really comfortable with him. By now, the buyer should not be withholding any information. If he does, it indicates one or both of the following: there is poor chemistry, or the buyer is playing games and may not be serious after all.

Since Bernie's chemistry with Bob is good, let's see if he will agree to coach him through the sale:

Bernie: Bob, you know Ms. Jones better than I do. What do you think she'll be interested in seeing or hearing when I meet with her?

Bob: Vicky isn't all that interested in details. My experience is that she likes to do business with people who are very concise and direct about how they can help us. She's very open-minded to input from people outside of the business, though she hates know-it-alls.

I think the best way to sell her is to bring with you the people who will be working on the audit. She's very conscious about the chemistry we have in our office, and won't want to hire anyone that she doesn't perceive as fitting in. I don't think it would hurt to make sure to include some women on your audit team because she is sensitive to women's issues and progression in the professions.

Bernie: How about slides or flip charts?

Bob: I don't think she likes fluff or glitz; she's much more interested in results. I'll leave that up to you. Don't expect her to read through some novel-length proposal. She hates paper-generators.

Wow! That's some very powerful input from someone who knows how the final decision-maker has made decisions in the past. You can see where Bernie could really err in this instance if he produced a male-dominated audit team and a flashy and lengthy presentation. And what presentation do you think Ms. Jones will most likely buy? The one that she wants to see or Bernie's standard presentation?

Now Bernie needs to jockey for last position:

Bernie: Bob, I have a request. I hope you have found our meeting as productive as I have. Can I touch base with you before you make your final cut to see where we stand?

Bob: Give me a call on Friday afternoon.

Again, if Bernie can't talk with Bob before he makes a final decision on the cut, this is a danger signal. If he does talk to him after he has interviewed all of the other firms, he has accomplished being last.

Plus, if Bernie is not one of the finalists, perhaps there was a misunderstanding. During that call, he can find out specifically why he wasn't chosen and then try to resolve these issues in order to make the final cut.

One key to a successful sale is to maintain more contact with the prospective client than your competition does. Use these contacts to show the prospective buyer your exceptional service and to give them lots of tender loving care.

After the sales call, Bernie will immediately write a personal thank-you note and send it attached to his firm brochure (which he had left back in the office, as was instructed earlier in Chapter 6). Now is also a good time for Bernie to check out the books and get to know Bob's staff. He'll find out what hurts they have that Bob isn't aware of.

Bernie can forward any information to Bob that he thinks he might be interested in; for example, a recent article about his industry. The more contact he has with Bob's business and staff without being a nuisance, the better. Chances are very good that his competition won't do anything between their interview and the cut date.

Please think about how this strategy could work for you. If you're an engineer, you should talk to the general contractor or other people you would interact with on the job. If you're a graphic designer, you could make a separate appointment to see what some of the company's existing collateral material looks like. If you're a computer consultant, you'd take a thorough look at the prospect's systems to see what kind of reports they are producing and what their backup situation is, as well as talk to some of the in-house staff about their problems with the system. Try to see how these analogies apply to you, instead of looking at how they can't apply to your own situation. You'll succeed much more if you follow the sales examination to the best of your ability, rather than say, "It wouldn't work for me."

Another Buying Scenario

In the previous discussion we reviewed a likely course of action in a competitive situation. However, sometimes you may be fortunate enough to be referred or invited into a business by the CEO, owner, or manager who is planning to meet only with you. That decision-making process is very different. Be prepared to secure that client immediately!

The biggest problem professional service providers have in the selling situation is that they don't know when the sale is made. When you are in front of decision-makers with whom you have good chemistry, who hurt, who are committed to action, and who will pay your fees, they are in a position to do something now. Although you personally might not take action without thinking it over for two-and-a-half weeks, people who run businesses make dynamic decisions all of the time.

If you're prepared to secure the client without a lengthy research and analysis process and without putting together a proposal, you will be able to make some sales in the decision step, even without a presentation.

Be prepared. In this situation the following will occur only if you are comfortable and ready for it:

Consultant: John, what does the decision-making process look like for hiring our firm?
John: Let's do it.

Close that deal on a handshake and get someone in there immediately to start work (that afternoon would be best). Stop back with an engagement agreement on your way home from the office, if that is normal for your business. Don't let their existing service-providers weasel their way back in.

Knocking Out the Competition

We move ahead to Friday afternoon as our hero, Bernie, calls to find out how the interviews with his competitors went:

Bernie: Bob? Hi! It's Bernie Fast. How are you?
Bob: Good, Bernie, and you?
Bernie: Fine, thanks. I'm calling to find out where we stand and how your interviews with the other firms went.
Bob: Sure. We've narrowed it down to you, Joe Blow & Co., and Young & Olde.
Bernie: Good! What happened with the other firms?
Bob: Dupers was far too big for us. We would have been a tiny fish in a massive pond. Arneson was kind of stuffy. Jack Sprat doesn't

do audits anymore, and Yours, Mine and Ours cancelled their appointment.
Bernie: Will you be rescheduling them?
Bob: No.

Bernie's reduced the competition down to two other firms. Now he may be able to knock out some more of the competition and see exactly where he stands:

Bernie: Bob, based on what you know so far and if we weren't involved in this process, between Joe Blow and Young & Olde, who would you recommend?

This is a powerful question, that Bernie must take the risk of asking. Once again, his competition (and very few others the buyer has come in contact with) have thought to ask it. Should Bernie be afraid to raise the issue? Why? He has good chemistry with Bob and the answer will help him immensely in the sales process.

One of my personal disappointments in selling is not asking the questions I know I would have asked, had I not been afraid. Don't go to your grave wondering what would have happened in your life, career, business, personal relationships, and finances if you had merely had the courage to ask the questions you wanted to ask but were afraid to, at the time!

Back to the conversation:

Bob: Joe Blow.

Kaboom! With one question Bernie has knocked out 50 percent of his competition. What started out as a fishing expedition with seven firms, is now narrowed down to him and one competitor. But Bernie still needs some more information:

Bernie: Was there anything about Young & Olde that would cause you to eliminate them?
Bob: They're the size firm I feel we need to handle our problems, but I can't say I really cared for the people they brought to the interview. All they did was babble on about how great they are; I don't think they asked more than a couple of questions about our situation. They're lousy listeners, too.

That's good knowledge to have about competition.

Bernie: Why would you select Joe Blow?

Bob: As you know, he's our current accountant. Joe is a really nice guy, and he's already familiar with our business.

Bernie: Why would you switch then? (Bernie would have discovered this information in Step 2, but it's good to have the buyer say it again.)

Bob: It's just him and a couple of support people. He really doesn't have the expertise to help us with our computer systems, cash management, inventory problems, collections, and so on. Joe's a great accountant, but that's about it; we need someone bigger. I'm tired of having to constantly search for outside help. And the bank wants more than just a sole practitioner's name on the financial statements.

Bob is the user decision-maker in this case. If Bernie was not able to get in front of Ms. Jones, Bob would also be the intermediate decision-maker. In that case, Bernie would have to elicit what Bob's decision would be as if he were the final decision-maker, because he would be empowered to sell his choice to Ms. Jones. It also will help to find out that information in this situation, as well:

Bernie: Bob, I don't want to be too direct, but if the choice were up to you alone, who would you be going with?

Bob: Of course I can't speak for Ms. Jones, but your firm appears best suited to fulfill our needs. And you've certainly followed through.

Oooh, that feels good: a job well done! However, Bernie must now secure the last appointment with Bob and Ms. Jones to sell her, too.

Bernie: Have you set the follow-up appointments with the other two firms?

Bob: No. I haven't notified them yet that they have been selected.

Bernie: Okay. Because new issues may arise in their meetings with you and Ms. Jones, I request that you set their appointments first; I would appreciate it very much if we could be last. That would give me the opportunity to address those issues that are certain to come up in those other meetings. When should I get back to you to find out when they're scheduled to come in?

Bob: I'll contact them on Monday. Call me Tuesday.
Bernie: Great. Thanks Bob, have a nice weekend.
Bob: You, too, Bernie.

Once again, one need not be afraid to request the last position. Asking to be last is expected and respected by experienced and smart buyers. Besides, Bernie has very good chemistry, and Bob is his advocate. It behooves him to help Bernie get hired.

Another possibility (usually not thought of by your competition):

Bernie: Okay. Because new issues may arise in their meetings with you and Ms. Jones, I request that you set their appointments first. I would appreciate it very much if we could be last. When should I get back to you to find out when they're scheduled to come in?
Bob: Joe Blow has already done that. We feel obligated to meet with him last because he's been with us so long.

Now Bernie would have trouble. Joe Blow is going to plead, cry, and beg not to lose his best client—and sometimes that works! Bernie needs to do one heck of a job in the presentation step to make sure Blow doesn't keep this client.

Bernie: How does Ms. Jones feel about that?
Bob: I don't know. But she's fond of old Joe.

Look out below! Bernie's prepared, though. He'll just have to jockey for last once more when he gets to the presentation step.

Diagnosis and Rx: Study the Anatomy of The Decision-Making Process

▸ You will want to thoroughly examine the decision-making process in order to facilitate your sale. This examination will help you to determine the flow of the decision, avoid wasting time, acquire a mentor, possibly eliminate your competition, and jockey for last position.
▸ There are six basic personality types you need to be concerned with. They are the following:

1. The leader: confident, direct, loves challenges, willing to take charge and go into action

2. The executive manager: motivated by personal gain, security, and looking good to others
3. The socializer: very amiable, has lots of friends, enjoys working with others, and loves personal attention
4. The overseer: resists change, motivated by what's best for the "family," selfless
5. The innovator: very novel and flexible, always looking for more time to create, eager to delegate responsibility for business matters
6. The accountant/engineer: extremely suspicious and conservative by nature, meticulous, wants to get the best value, very slow to make a decision

Knowing what type of personality you're dealing with will help you guide the decision-making process in your favor. You can quickly size up people by their behavior, position in the company, and office environment.

▸ The way in which you make decisions will affect the way you get decisions. Most business leaders are used to and prefer making speedy decisions. Therefore, you should practice making quick decisions, so you can get a similar response from prospects. Stop thinking things over and just do it.

▸ Your examination will be complete when you have the answers to these four questions:

1. Who are the decision-makers?
2. Who is the competition?
3. When will the decision be made?
4. How will the decision be made?

▸ In many instances, the decision-making process is not straightforward. There are five separate parties who may participate in a decision; these are the following:

1. The money man (or woman)
2. The user
3. The outside intruder (whoever the buyer turns to for business advice)
4. The intermediate
5. Committees

To succeed, you must find out exactly how many of these parties are involved in the decision, and do your best to sell each participant individually.

▸ Throughout the sale, show your prospective client a high level of attention and service. Send a personal thank-you note and relevant literature. Talk to the prospect's staff to uncover any new issues that might be relevant. Be involved, but stop short of becoming a nuisance.

▸ Remember that business leaders are used to making swift decisions. Be prepared to close the sale quickly; don't keep selling when you should be finalizing the close.

10

Looking Good And Locking It Up in The One-Call Sale

In this chapter, you'll be guided through the delicate and sometimes dangerous presentation and proposal process. You'll discover how to give more successful presentations and/or proposals and how to achieve the one-call sale. This covers Step 6: Test to See If a Presentation or Proposal Is Necessary, and Determine What It Should Look Like.

Is a Presentation or Proposal Really Necessary?

Testing the presentation and proposal process will enable you to:

1. *Do as little work as possible and still get the business.* Work smart, not hard!

2. *Satisfy the buyers' intellectual needs.* People buy for emotional reasons, but they need to intellectually justify their purchases to the left side of their brain (the emotional sphere), as well as to their superiors, subordinates, spouses, relatives, friends, and others. In this step you will give buyers the justifications they need to buy.

Some people don't need to have logical considerations to buy; they've already sold themselves. That's why you need to test to see if a presentation or a proposal is necessary. If you insist on giving a presentation or doing a proposal when one isn't necessary, the odds increase dramatically that you will lose a sale that you would have otherwise made.

3. *Give the buyer the opportunity to ask you questions.* Thus far, you've been conducting a sales interview, with the buyer supplying the information you need to determine if you want to proceed. This step is where the buyer should be asking you questions (if any).

4. *Avoid wasting time and effort and giving away free ideas.* Creating winning presentations and proposals can be extremely time-consuming and difficult. Your time to market and sell is limited and valuable, and it should be invested only in those situations where you have the greatest likelihood of success for the kind of business you want.

Some buyers really aren't buyers at all and look upon the presentation and proposal process as a way to get free advice. That's why you've conducted due diligence to this point in the sale to determine if you have a real buyer on your hands or not. Little feels worse than discovering your prospects were really suspects who took your ideas to give them to their current service-providers or simply put your advice into action themselves. Proceed with extreme caution if you feel you have a browser or a freeloader as a buyer.

5. *Give a custom-designed presentation or proposal (if necessary) that the buyer wants to see.* If you've determined that a presentation or proposal is necessary, then you should prepare and present only that which the buyer will purchase. Two often professional service-providers go back to their offices and agonize over what the proposal or presentation should look like—without asking the buyer for their input! The buyer is most likely to purchase that which she helped construct. In this chapter, we will discuss how to create a presentation or a proposal that the buyer wants to see.

6. *Avoid talking yourself out of a sale.* You must always be cognizant of the positive and negative emotional swings buyers can go through during the selling cycle. If your buyers are positive, they are in a dangerous position because they only have one direction in which to swing: negative. This is how so many people talk themselves out of sales: the buyer was positive but proceeded to the negative as the professional service provider kept talking and oversold.

Also, if the buyers are negative, should you be presenting or proposing to them in the first place? Because you are in control of the sales process, you can decide if you have a good shot at getting the business. It wouldn't hurt in the negative or neutral situation to ask the buyer that question.

How to Perform Step 6: The Transition from Step 5

Let's review where you are in the sale:

- You and the prospective client have been developing a rapport and chemistry with each other.
- The client is telling you his emotional needs, wants, desires, and musts, as well as the background information necessary for you to diagnose the situation.
- The buyer is committed to action.
- You are comfortable with the buyer's willingness to pay your fees.
- You've discovered the decision-making process, determined your ability to influence this process, and positioned yourself for the best possible advantage.

Now you need to address the presentation process. If you have conducted the sales examination correctly, your closing ratio should be approximately ninety percent or more from this point forward.

The Informal Presentation

Most professional service providers reading this book should be concerned with mastering the informal presentation. Informal presentations apply to individual clients and to very small to medium-size companies that are not going to go through an exhaustive formalized process to make a decision.

The One-Call Sale Scenario

You're in front of the owner or decision-makers. You've been conducting a sales examination interview by asking questions, and they've done 80 percent or more of the talking. There's good chemistry, you know where it hurts, and you have cleared fees. Be prepared to close the sale and leave with a new client today!

The sales examination process was designed to have your prospective client feel safe and extremely positive by this time--unlike a typical sales call. If you leave without securing a decision, the client will have only one way to go: to the neutral or negative on the emotional swing.

At this point in the process, it's time to satisfy the buyers' intellectual needs by inviting them to ask you questions.

Consultant: Harry, thanks for filling me in about your situation. What questions do you have for me?

The buyer will not ask you those questions he needs answered to satisfy his intellectual needs. Be prepared—some buyers will say that you have already answered their questions. If so, proceed immediately to the final step in the sales examination: formalization and closure (see Chapter 13).

Many buyers, however, will ask you some questions at this point, although not necessarily as many as you thought they would nor as many as you might, given a role reversal. Be very careful in this step as there are two possible reactions to everything you say or propose: the buyer will either like it or dislike it. Those are dangerous odds!

In order to avoid talking yourself out of the sale, remember:

• *Who you are talking to and what you are talking about.* To be most effective in your presentation, you must respond in the appropriate way to the type of decision-maker you are talking to. Each type of decision-maker has different needs to be met (see Chapter 9 for review). Also, you must relate what you say to where it hurts. Your presentation is the time to tell the buyer, now that he has qualified, how you can ease his aches. Be sure and reflect upon your detailed notes before you speak.

• *Get to the point; don't ramble on.* People get bored easily. Too often sales are lost because the seller turns an easily answered question into a long-winded dissertation. The buyer gets bored, swings to neutral or negative, and the sale is lost.

• *Tell stories (mini-case histories) to back up your claims.* Information can be dry and may easily bore the buyer. Also, whatever you say about yourself is pure conjecture on your part. Lend credibility and spice to your presentations by backing up what you say about you and your firm with references to similar situations you and/or the firm have handled successfully. Because you took extensive notes during the conversation, you should already be able to relate in some way the buyer's situation to something you have been involved with in the past. Answer the buyer's concerns using references to third parties.

• *Don't make claims you can't support.* The last thing you want to do is brag about some amazing achievement and not have the data to support your claims. Such behavior will cause you to instantly lose credibility with your prospective client and possibly even lose the sale. When providing information, make sure that what you say is what the client wants to hear, and that you can support your claims with at least one real-life example that directly proves your point.

• *Don't answer unasked questions unless you know for a fact that the client must hear about it.* If you ever hear the words "Oh, by the way . . ." coming from your mouth, you are in deep trouble. Everything you say can and will be held against you.

In the section that follows, you will see how to present to the leader personality types on a one-call sale. You will observe two totally distinct sales scenarios: the first involves a marketing consultant, and the second, an accountant. Although these fields are totally different by the very nature of the services they provide and by the kinds of people who inhabit these professions, note the similarity in purpose and result.

Presenting to the Leader Decision-Maker: Scenario 1

Consultant: Stella, thanks for filling me in about your situation. What questions do you have for me?

Stella: Chloe, tell me what you are going to do that will help me in my real estate business.

Consultant: Just to recap, you mentioned that the market for single-family homes is improving and that you are doing quite well, but you don't feel that you are getting your share of the business considering that the firm has been established here in Hokum City for fifteen years.

You're spending a fortune on advertising but not getting the results you used to for the dollars being spent. When the phone rings, some of your agents don't pick it up, and most have difficulty closing sales that should be easily sold. Your arch-rival competitor, Slokum Realty, is taking market share from you and has changed their marketing, but you're not quite sure how. Also, they seem to have better salespeople working for them.

You've been doing all of the market-related functions for your office all of these years, but it's become simply too much for you as you realize that you need to get back into the community and out there selling yourself. The other marketing consultants that you've talked to don't appear to have much expertise in your field, although they say they do. Over the next three-to-five years, you'd like to build the business up so that you can be in a position to sell if you like, to semi-retire and take it easier. Did I miss anything?

Stella: No, you're doing fine.

Consultant: Our firm ran into a similar situation a couple of years back with another real estate office over in East Rogers Park. Of course, you'll remember that was in a down market because of the economy. Do you know Thelma Thrasher over at XYZ Realty? She doesn't mind us mentioning her as a referral source or discussing the situation that led her to be our client.

Although no legitimate marketing consultants could promise you instantaneous results, we've been able to improve Thelma's market share by 38 percent in the last two years, and XYZ Realty wasn't a small firm to begin with, as you know.

We shifted her advertising program away from strictly newspaper ads and gave her an integrated program using different forms of media to multiply the effect, without increasing her advertising budget. Like you, Thelma was in charge of the company's marketing; now she's turned almost all of it over to us so that she can concentrate on those things she feels are absolute priorities. In her case, she trains each salesperson personally by monitoring their phone conversations, going on sales appointments, and even showing them how to get listings on the phones and door-to-door. That's what she loves to do.

Stella: I don't have the patience for that.

Consultant: In your case then, we would bring in a sales expert that we've worked with in the past to set up a training program for your people and then install a sales reporting system so that you and we could track exactly what these people are doing. It's possible that you have some deadwood here.

Stella: My goodness, yes.

Consultant: We've found that the best salespeople want to work for whom they perceive as the best real estate companies. Working for the best companies enhances their opportunities for more sales, since these companies generally have more powerful advertising and more leads coming in. You and I will sit down and set our goals for your firm's growth of market share. We'll find out what it is right now and then track it monthly with you to make sure you are absolutely delighted with us as our client.

Our goal will be to build your business to where you want it to be so that you will be in a position in three-to-five years to sell a phenomenally successful market leader, should you want to. Only by having delighted clients can we get referrals to our next clients. We need and expect our happy clients to help us build our business.

What other questions do you have?

Stella: I worked with a marketing consultant once before, and mostly what I got out of the relationship was a thinner bank account. She promised some of the things you have, but nothing changed. How do I kow that you're not making empty promises too?

Consultant: Stella, I'm in business just like you. If I go around making promises I can't keep, my clients won't be any happier with me than you are with that other consultant. Repeat business is the name of your business and mine. You'll be right back on the street looking for someone else, saying that I promised and couldn't deliver.

However, there is no scientific way to obtain market share and accomplish what you want. The results may not happen tomorrow. We've found that marketing always works, when it is done correctly. It must be a sustained and managed effort. We'll do everything we can to help you reach your goals—that's how we've become as successful as we are.

If I didn't think we could help you, I would have told you right away. That's one reason we're not going to be cheaper than other marketing consultants here in Hokum City or in the region. I'm excited by the possibilities you have here; I think there is tremendous potential.

What other questions do you have for me in order for us to get started?

Stella: I can't think of anything else. What you've said sounds wonderful. Let's get started. I look forward to working with you.

Presenting to the Leader Decision-Maker: Scenario 2

Accountant: Harry, thanks for filling me in about your situation. What questions do you have for me?

Harry: Tom, tell me what you are going to do that will help me in my business.

Accountant: You mentioned that your current accountant is slow to get you the financial statements and slow to respond to your phone calls, sometimes taking two or more days to get back to you. Also, she really doesn't know anything about your industry. Is that correct?

Harry: Yes.

Accountant: We ran into a similar situation about two months ago with another company about your size in a different industry. Perhaps you know Joe Dokes over at ABC International? He doesn't mind us mentioning him as a referral source or discussing the situation that led him to be our client.

Although no CPA firm can promise you instantaneous financial statements, we've been able to improve the response time to Joe by about 80 percent. We're able to get him the information he needs when he needs it for his bank, too. Because Joe's been negotiating with his banker for a better interest rate and a new line of credit, Joe had us sit down and explain the comparative financials to him and his banker line by line. He also wanted us to help him make faster and better decisions in a down market. He's told me that his banker is very happy about working with us, and she has referred us to several of her clients, as well.

Regarding our response time to our clients' inquiries, I'm quite proud of it. Because we're not always in our office, we've installed a new voice mail system that allows our clients to access us at any time and leave a detailed message. This allows us to check into a matter that might be concerning you, research it, and get back to you faster. My clients have told me it has helped them make better use of their time, too.

We know that our clients use our information to better manage their companies. We're set up to help them do just that in areas besides accounting and auditing as well. Because we have an ongoing relationship, we know our clients better than any other service provider possibly could. When the need arises, we're right there to help them with their computer problems, with inventory control guidance, cash management ideas, and health benefits consulting, for example.

What other questions do you have?

Harry: Our last two CPAs also promised great response time, but we keep running into the same problem. How do I know that you're not just making empty promises, too?

Accountant: Harry, I'm in business just like you. If I go around making promises I can't keep, my clients won't be any happier with me than your customers are with you when your deliveries aren't on time. If I don't deliver, you'll be right back on the street looking for another CPA, saying that I promised and couldn't deliver.

However, there are going to be times when we might not be able to get back to you as quickly as we'd like, and that's why I asked what your conditions of satisfaction were before we started.

You told me that you'd be satisfied if we got back to you within four hours of a phone call, and if we could get your financial statements to you within twenty days of the end of the month. If I didn't think we could do that, I would've stopped you right there. That's one reason we're not going to be cheaper than your current CPAs or anyone else, and we may be more expensive. We've invested in our office and staff for excellent client response.

However, to fulfill these promises, we'll also need the cooperation of your people. And there are times when I'm traveling or simply unable to respond that quickly, which I hope you'll understand. My hope is that you'll work with us as your partner. If you ever have a problem or concern, we need to discuss it immediately.

I need delighted clients like you to refer me to other people in similar situations who might need my help as well. That's how we've grown our practice. If you're not satisfied, I've just wasted both our time, and neither of us can afford that.

What other questions do you have?

Harry: Good. Let's do it and get it over with.

Comparing the Presentations

Please note that these two presentations, to different people from people selling dramatically different services, are essentially the same. Professional services have characteristics in common, no matter what the particular service is:

- They are all intangible.
- The sale hinges on the individual service provider's interaction with the buyer.
- You need to separate yourself clearly from the competition because there is nothing for the buyer to see, feel, hear, touch, or smell; you are the only indication the buyer has of the quality of the service you are offering.

Note that both of these presentations were to the point. Although they may have been lengthy to read, in each instance the presentation might have taken a maximum of only ten minutes.

Presenting to the Executive/Manager Decision-Maker

Here is a scenario where you will again observe the sale of marketing consulting, this time to an executive decision-maker—not a leader. Note the differences:

Consultant: Karen, thanks for filling me in about your situation. What questions do you have for me?

Karen: Tell me what you are going to do that will help our real estate business.

Consultant: We started our conversation by discussing your eighteen offices in a three-county area. Each unit is in its own distinct marketplace. Although some are located in the same county, they are in different locations within that county, which could reflect totally different demographics for each locale.

    The idea to eliminate the in-house marketing function wasn't yours, but rather the board of directors', which is really the family of the founder of the company. They want to cut costs and will hold you responsible for outsourcing the marketing function and the results of the firm you hire. Market share is down somewhat, and you want to work with people who can work well with you personally, as you will be overseeing marketing. Each office's manager will want to have input about the marketing for his or her office, but the ultimate decisions will be yours. You were hired away from another large firm and have been president for three years, but you don't have a marketing background. Did I miss anything?

Karen: That covers it pretty well.

Consultant: We ran into a similar situation a few years ago in the northern part of the state. Perhaps you know Selma Salmon of the Fish Realty Company in Pompano Pines?

Karen: Sure, I've known Selma for years from the state board of realtors.

Consultant: She doesn't mind us using her as a referral source or discussing the situation that led to her becoming our client. Like you, she was hired by a family-owned company whose business had outgrown them. She was the third president they'd had in three years. Her firm had twelve offices and no marketing function whatever. The family that owned it held her responsible for everything; finally, she was able to persuade them that she needed to hire a marketing firm to help out.

Selma had seen one of my partners speak at a realtor's association meeting on the subject of investing marketing dollars for maximum payoff, so she called him in and they hired us immediately.

We started with Selma's firm by putting together their first marketing plan and then developing the strategy to carry it out—including the where and when of investing their advertising dollars. We came in and trained her people and set up a new incentive and bonus system. We rewrote their brochures to make them state-of-the-art, as well as redesigned all of their ads and collateral material to bring it into the 1990s. We installed a sales management system so that she can monitor activities weekly by office.

Within a year of working with us, their return on the investment was about twelve to one; profits really increased, as did market share. Selma herself got a new five-year contract, a piece of the business, and a substantial raise. She was so happy that she introduced us to four other state real estate associations, and we've been able to take our business national.

Karen: I can't afford to hire the wrong people.

Consultant: Of course you can't—but you have to understand that we will need to work together closely so we can get up-to-speed as quickly as possible. Although we'll be doing the work, we need your constant input and the freedom to talk to your office managers and salespeople in order to get a better feel for the market and ensure the success of the project.

I think the biggest mistake firms make when they hire us is to look at it as a short-term relationship. Smart companies realize they need us as their outside experts to monitor results objectively and to be the people who constantly bring them new ideas. We look for that long-term relationship. We really act as an insurance policy to secure the future of the business and the employees by helping to facilitate increased success. And we also need the help of our delighted clients to bring us business through referrals as we bring them business.

I know you want to save money over the in-house marketing function, and you really don't need a full-time staff to do this. Our fee represents a small amount of your whole advertising expense and the results you need.

What other questions do you have?

Karen: Let's get started.

Presenting to the Socializer Decision-Maker

Consultant: Larry, thanks for filling me in about your situation. What do we need to talk about in order for us to move forward and get started?

Larry: You know I really like our current architect. Is there some way we can keep her involved?

Consultant: Based on what you've told me, she seems like a genuinely nice person. It's unfortunate you haven't been able to have the attention and relationship you'd hoped for from her.

As a rule, we don't work with other architects unless they have a certain expertise we don't possess, or the client has project sites spread out all over the place. In those cases where it's economically practical, we'd rather work with old friends in that particular city—people we know who can do the best job.

Maybe you should keep her on and have her switch the staff architects again.

Larry: No, I've tried that! I hired her for her personal attention to our projects, but she insists on leveraging down to these junior people and ignoring me. Hey, how are you going to be any different?

Consultant: We ran into a similar situation with Jim Shoe over at Walk and Talk Shoe Company. He and I have become very close, and he doesn't mind when I tell about his situation. Perhaps you know him?

Larry: Sure. He's been around for years. I see him at the club.

Consultant: Like you, Jim has an expanding business that requires constant construction of new plants and offices. He had an architect who he thought would devote a lot of personal attention to him. They hit it off right away. Basically, that was the last time he saw the guy!

Larry, I look for clients to bring into the firm who I feel I can develop a long-term relationship with. But you need to understand that I am not the person that will actually be doing the day-to-day work, just like you're not in the back room making cold telephone calls anymore. My plans are to secure you as a client and then meet with you on a regularly scheduled basis to discuss the projects and maintain and improve our relationship. That's why I asked you earlier for your conditions of satisfaction.

We need to stay in touch by talking on the phone as often as we both feel the need to. You'll have access to me if I'm not in the office via our voice mail system or by using my beeper.

And I'll be around to keep tabs on my people, to make sure

the work is of high quality and to maintain my relationship with them. My goal is that they will develop solid connections with your people on the project.

Meeting and talking regularly will also give us the opportunity to discuss any areas that affect the construction of the project as a whole and to make sure your relationships with your contractors, your employees, and the others involved stay strong. We want to stay on top of your situation to make sure your relationships with the people who will be working in these facilities are kept secure.

I need strong alliances with clients like you to refer us to other people who might not have the kind of relationships they want with their architect. That's how I've built my circle of clients.

Have you thought about how you will dismiss the other architect?

Larry: Well, no, but I'm sure I can handle it.

Consultant: Please let me take care of that for you. I'll give her a call immediately and set up a meeting with her to transfer the job from her offices; it's done all of the time. You won't have a thing to worry about, and I'll explain the situation to her as kindly as I can. Perhaps she can learn from this experience for her own benefit.

Larry: That would be much appreciated.

Presenting to the Overseer Decision-Maker

Consultant: Ben, thanks for filling me in about your situation here on the ranch. What questions do you have for me?

Ben: Tom, tell me who's going to work on our account. We don't want to do anything that'll upset the chemistry we have around here.

Consultant: Earlier you mentioned that your current computer consultant is not the person you hired—in the sense that you never see her. Since the day she was hired, you've been stuck with a myriad of rotating junior staff people; it's like having strangers around all the time. The constant changes make everyone uncomfortable. And none of the staff people are really up-to-speed on your equipment or systems.

We ran into a similar situation with Jan Doe over at XYZ Agri-National. She and I have become good friends, and she doesn't mind when I tell her story.

Like your group, she hired a computer consultant who she

thought would fit in perfectly with her people. At first, she accepted the people the firm was sending out because she wanted to give her contact person a chance. But the other consultant dropped the ball, took her for granted, and ignored the relationship. Jan almost lost one of her best accounts-receivable clerks because the staff person was talking down to him.

Fortunately, she was introduced to us. She's been so happy with our people that she has referred about eight new clients to us in the past year.

Ben, you need to understand that I am not the person that will actually be doing the day-to-day work on the computers—just like you're not out in the fields herding cattle. My plans are to bring you into our client family, and then have you and your office staff meet some of our people who will be working on your project, so everyone can start feeling comfortable with each other. Of course, I have confidence in all of our people to get the job done right, and I realize everyone won't meld into your environment in the same way.

Is that okay?

Ben: Sounds fine. But what about our work with you? Surely a staff person can't meet all of our needs—you're the person I want to interact with.

Consultant: And you will. You and I will be meeting on a regular basis for lunch or in your office to discuss exactly what's going on and to make sure everything is going smoothly. We'll be in regular communication, and I'll be controlling the quality of our staff's work.

Meeting and talking regularly will also give us the opportunity to discuss any areas outside of computer consulting, such as better inventory-control systems and improved cash-management systems, to help make sure the company is running as efficiently and profitably as possible. This will benefit everyone. We want to stay on top of your computer situation to make sure your customers and office staff are kept happy; we hope you will see us as part of your corporate family. We want to benefit everyone around here.

As far as working with me, you can access me at any time, almost as well as if I were right here on the job. If I'm not in my office, you can access my voice mail system or my beeper, and I'll get back to you right away.

Ben, I have a responsibility to the people on my team—just like you do for yours—to look out for their best interests. If I go around making promises I can't keep, my clients won't be any happier with me than your customers are with you when your deliveries aren't on time. You'd be looking again outside of the relationship for another computer consulting firm. We don't want to lose anyone from our client family.

However, we'll need the cooperation of your people too, to accomplish our goals. And there are times when I'm traveling or simply unable to respond that quickly, which I hope you'll understand. My hope is that you'll see us as a member of your family. If there is a problem, we can discuss it immediately.

We need delighted clients like you to refer us to other folks in similar situations who might need our help as well. That's how we've built our team. We know that we're responsible to our clients and our staff to manage the business properly so they don't have to worry about continuity or job stability.

What other questions do you have before we set up a meeting with your staff and my people to get started?

Ben: Fine. Let's set a date to get our staffs together here in our conference room. We'll bring lunch in and make it informal.

Presenting to the Innovator Decision-Maker

Consultant: Ariel, thanks for sketching out your situation here. What do we need to review in order for us to take these problems off your hands and free you up for what you'd rather be doing?

Ariel: My last business manager and agent wasn't responsible at all, and he was an attorney! He left a lot of detail up to me, and I'm not a business person—you've probably been able to see that by now. I need someone to help me keep an eye on the business, to negotiate my contracts, and to help me avoid making bad business decisions.

Consultant: That's one reason we'll be more expensive than your current agent. We want to deliver the service that you need to continue to be profitable and grow your business and career.

Some clients only want us to be very slightly involved; others turn total control of their careers over to us. I don't think that's necessary here. Of course, the level of service dictates our fees.

Your situation is very similar to one I encountered when I first started in managing people's businesses years ago, although they were in a different industry. Our client was an interior design firm. They were known all over the East Coast for their work. Unfortunately, they didn't know or care a thing about running a profitable business; therefore, they were sitting ducks for the government and were always running into situations they couldn't see their way out of. We became their trusted business advisors, and they referred us to dozens of their artistic friends who also weren't inclined to run businesses.

Ariel, I wouldn't want to bring you in as a client unless I knew we could help you. We've created our firm with clients like you who have shown us the way to their counterparts.

Now, can we get started so you can get back to those projects you'd rather be working on?

Presenting to the Accountant/Engineer Decision-Maker

Consultant: Will, thanks for filling me in about your situation. What do we need to review in order for us to move forward and start?

Will: As you know, I used to work for Blood and Guts, CPAs. I know everything about accounting and how you guys try to run up your bills. I believe CPAs are generic, especially on audits, and I want the best bang for our buck. I know how much partners make—I don't want you getting rich off of me or my company.

Consultant: As we discussed earlier, we're definitely not going to be the cheapest firm. And we won't cut corners to get any engagement. Our goal is not to wind up in court as defendants in a negligence suit because we took a client in that we couldn't afford to service properly. If you are still looking for the cheapest accountants you can find, there are probably others out there who will take that risk. We also believe that we should make a fair profit.

We invest almost 5 percent of gross revenues in training our partners and staff to keep up-to-date on what is a very changeable profession—as you know.

We run into similar situations all the time where prospective clients are looking for the "biggest bang for their buck." The most recent situation was a new client who chose a firm whose fees were approximately two-thirds of our estimate. They saw auditing services as generic, too.

Usually, people get what they pay for. Because the fees were so low, their previous accountants assigned very inexperienced people who were improperly managed, and the effect was to delay the audit by six weeks. In this economy, the bankers got nervous and the shareholders and board weren't too pleased. And the client was losing control over her job because she was constantly training the junior people from the accounting firm.

Because the firm was so rushed to get the work out, the numbers were wrong, there were typographical errors, and the financial statements were not only late but also had to be rescinded and then reissued. Unfortunately, the person that thought she was doing her best by hiring the cheapest firm caught the heat on that one. The CPA firm was fired immediately and we got a new client.

Frankly, I can't understand why companies insist on saving a relatively minor amount of money off of their bottom line. At the time, the amount may look like a lot of money dollar for dollar, but this relatively small savings then winds up putting their business, and the shareholders, banking, and board of director relationships at risk. In that situation, for a lousy $7,000, they almost lost their new line of credit and a good interest rate they worked years to get.

Will: Are you promising then to have all of your work done no later than when I want it?

Consultant: Will, if we decide to work together, then we're going to have to create a partnership. As you know, there are times of the year when we'll be more pressed for time than others. Especially you are aware of that; you remember the ninety-hour weeks during the busy season!

If we move ahead, we'll work closely to ensure that you get the quality of work you need in a time frame we can both live with. But we'll need the utmost cooperation of your staff as well. I can't uphold my end if your people hold us back. We'll do everything we can to leverage off your people to save you fees and speed up the process.

Will: We don't want any disruptions in our regular activities.

Consultant: Nor do we. However, as you know, auditors can't be totally invisible during the audit process. We need access to you and information. We'll try to keep disruptions to a minimum.

What other questions do you have?

Will: Our current accountants are always bothering me about buying more of their high-priced services. I don't like that.

Consultant: Times have changed. Our firm no longer comes in to a company once a year and then leaves. Our people are trained to keep their eyes open for problems or improvements that the client might not be aware of.

Our goal is to have healthy clients who pay our bills on time, and who refer us to their counterparts in other businesses. Because of that, we have developed expertise in areas that CPA firms traditionally haven't ventured into, such as computer selection and installation, health beneifts consulting, cash management consulting, and inventory control. Because you are already an expert CPA, you may not need any help in those areas beyond what you are doing now.

However, I will be coming to you on a regular basis to review the progress on the audit. If something is brought to my attention that I feel you should know about, I'm going to bring it up. I promise not to "sell" you or pressure you into doing anything you don't want or need to do. I'm more like a doctor in that, if we detect a problem, I will discuss with you how to get healthier. If you decide not to act on my input, so be it.

Will: How much expertise do you have in our business? We don't want to pay your people and train them as well.

Consultant: We don't have any direct experience in the thermoblaster industry, which also means we're not working with any of your competitors. However, we do have expertise in the turbobanger industry, which in many ways looks to be similar to yours. Our goal is not to gain experience at your cost. I expect our audit to cost no more, nor take any longer, than it normally would if we did thermoblaster audits all of the time. Of course, I will reserve the right to tap into your expertise in the industry and ask for guidance at times, if the need occurs. We must work as partners to produce the best end-result for you and your company.

And, based on what I've learned so far about your company, I think there's a good match to our existing expertise. We'd like to work with you, but I need to take a look at your records and get a better idea of what is involved before we can proceed formally. I'd like to meet your staff and see your systems.

Here's a written case study detailing a similar situation in the turbobanger industry. And here's the name of one of our clients who is ready to talk to you about our work with her in that industry. I request that you call her and scan our case study while I start reviewing your records and meeting your people.

Should we moving ahead?

Will: I want to know how you would handle the situation with the IRS that I mentioned earlier.

Consultant: You told me earlier what the other firms you've interviewed have suggested, and what your plans are. At this point, I

don't have enough information to make a recommendation that I
want to be held to.

    Why didn't you just go with one of their suggestions and
hire them?

Will: I didn't like their advice. I want your input now.

Consultant: Will, please excuse me for putting you off, but I simply
don't have enough background info to give you a decent opinion.
I haven't talked to my contacts at the IRS nor reviewed it with my
tax partner.

    All I can say is that I've successfully settled similar matters
in the past that my clients have been very pleased with. We had
a case about four months ago where the IRS had billed what became a new corporate client for back taxes, penalties, and interest
totalling over $100,000. It wasn't easy, but we researched it and
negotiated them down to something much more reasonable,
about $28,000, with the interest and penalties dismissed.

    If you decide to move ahead, I'll be happy to devote the same
resources to your situation as was dedicated to them. However, I
can't promise any such result for you, which I know you'll understand.

Will: Thanks for being straight with me. Let's go meet my staff.

That was a lot of work! Please note that in dealing with these
highly technical types of people, be prepared to be put through the
ringer when it comes to providing information and details about how
you are going to accomplish the project. All too often the service provider, no matter what he is selling, loses a sale that should've been
won because he wasn't willing to try to make this risk-averse type of
client comfortable. On the other hand, note that our hero didn't give
away lots of free ideas.

Some Observations about Your One-Call Sale

    1. *The informal presentation process should take a relatively short period
of time.* Up to this point the buyer has done approximately 80 percent
of the talking. You, as the professional service provider, have invested
your time in finding out about their business and have qualified them
to the best of your ability for their aches, your fees, and the process
for making a decision. In this informal, one-call sale scenario, you
should expect to leave with the business today.

    So much of your communication is not in your words but in the
way you act during the conversation. By taking notes, you've shown

that you were concerned, detail-oriented, and thorough. Your questioning strategy has allowed the buyer to feel comfortable and talk about his personal goals. Ninety percent of the sale has been made if you've conducted your sales examination correctly.

The presentation provides the intellectual information needed to satisfy the left side of the buyer's brain. Because you probably deal with more businesspeople than accountants or engineers, this need may be less than if you were the buyer. Your presentation might only take five minutes or so with many buyers.

Be careful! Professional service providers have the bad habit of putting their egoes first and making the sale second. Too often, professionals think they have to show how brilliant they are. They explain (talk) too much, thus blowing the sale because the buyer becomes bored stiff (as the emotional swing moves to the negative). That is how a seller can talk himself right out of a sale.

By employing the examination-process on your sales call, you won't bore the buyers to tears. If the buyers are properly qualified, their emotional swing is still in the positive position. Therefore, after your part of the sales interview—the informal presentation—you must be prepared to leave with a new client or a new piece of work from an existing client. Don't continue to sell after the sale is made!

2. *You, as the professional service provider, should direct your informal presentation to the type of person you are talking to.* By listening and observing the buyer carefully, you're able to custom-design your mini-presentation for the buyer.

In presenting to the leader, to the entrepreneur, you focus on results, not details. For the executive/manager, you tailor your presentation to focus on security, and what is in it for them. To the overseer, you should speak in terms of group welfare. In presenting to the socializer, you concentrate on the relationship aspects and handle the rejection problem. For the innovator, you free her from the burden of business and give her more time to create. And, finally, when presenting to the accountant/engineer, you provide a case study and a referral to talk to immediately, thereby proving value, providing details, lending credibility, and offering safety for a decision. Also, with each type of buyer, you relate whatever you said to where they hurt, and how you would ease their aches.

3. *You don't beg for the business.* So many professionals beg for the business because they don't know how to sell professional services. You present to the buyer the behavior of someone already very successful. People like dealing with successful people ("There must be a reason . . .") rather than someone in need.

4. *You should stick to the point and not ramble on.* People get bored very easily. Sales are often lost when the seller answers a simple question with a long diatribe of information. The buyer usually finds such dissertations quite uninteresting and may swing to a neutral or even negative position. Do your best to keep your answers short and simple.

5. *You should tell stories (case histories) to back up your claims.* Data can be dull and boring. To spice up your presentation, tell the buyer stories that illustrate the points you are trying to make. During the interview, as you take notes, you will likely hear aches that remind you of problems you've handled successfully in the past. When it's time for you to present, refer to these notes and share how you handled a similar situation. Backing up what you say with references to comparable situations that you and your firm handled successfully will give you great credibility with prospective buyers.

6. *You shouldn't make claims that you can't support.* Just as sharing relevant success stories will add to your credibility, making unsubstantiated claims can really harm your relationship with the buyer. If you spout off amazing statistics or achievements but have no concrete way to back them up, buyers are likely to become skeptical and suspicious. They may swing neutral or negative, costing you the sale.

7. *You don't answer unasked questions unless you know for a fact that the client must hear about it.* Offering too much information can only hurt you. By rambling on, you are likely to at least bore the buyer; in the worst case, you might even lose the sale. In the presentation step—when it's finally your turn to do the talking—you should be very careful to tell the buyer only what he has told you he wants to hear. Spice this data up with case histories that directly illustrate your points. And if you ever hear the words, "Oh, by the way . . ." coming from your mouth, you are in serious trouble. Anything you say can and will be held against you.

In the informal presentation, you should mention some of the additional services your firm offers to clients to help them operate their business more efficiently. Done early in the relationship process, this avoids the need to constantly educate the client and remind them later on about not going outside the relationship (to your competitors or third-party interlopers) to get their other business aches solved. In the future, your newsletters, communications, brochures, seminars, and conversations will further bring attention to and reinforce the full-service notion.

Selling Additional Services to Existing Clients

The only difference between selling business to new clients and selling new services to existing, satisfied clients is that selling to satisfied
clients should be easier. For example, you would be likely to get a
dental implant if your regular dentist suggested one to replace a problem tooth. If you believe that your dentist is knowledgeable and trust-
worthy—which you should, since he's your dentist—you would be
likely to rely on his judgment regarding additional services. The same
is true for selling more services to your existing clients: They are more
likely to buy from you, but only if they see you as an advisor, not just
their accountant or computer consultant.

Let's go to a sales scenario where the business management consultant has already discussed the aches of the current computer system with her client:

Consultant: Thanks for sharing with me about what's working and
not working with your existing computer system.

You said it's taking you longer and longer to get the information off the computer, information that you need to run your
business on a daily basis, and that shipments are being stalled
because of all of the patching that's going on. Overtime is higher
then ever in the computer department. Sounds like you've outgrown the system.

We've discussed our estimated fee for searching out an en-
hanced replacement system that we can then help you install.
What questions do you have for me?

Mike: Have you done this kind of work before? Don't you spend
most of your time just doing business consulting?

Consultant: Yes, our practice is still dominated by business and management consulting. But the needs of our clients have demanded
that we be proactive in their concerns with PCs, networks, and
replacing minis as well. We've been doing a lot of computer-re-
lated work these past five years, mostly with clients just like you.
We've found that, as your management consultants, we know
your business better than anyone else and can save you the trouble and time of having an outsider become familiar with your
business, systems, and personnel. We've found that outsiders
are more likely to propose inappropriate solutions resulting in
increased downtime, patching and rewriting programs, and retraining personnel, all of which they charge for handsomely.

Recently, we installed a Schwarzkopf X-94 over at Phillips

Hydromakers. They were in a similar situation to you. They wanted to replace an outdated minicomputer with the increased flexibility offered by a PC networking environment. We handled the entire hardware and software selection process, installation, and training of personnel, and we guided them in transferring the records over to the new system. They ran parallel for three months and were very pleased.

Mike: Good. Let's go talk to the DP manager and get started.

Consultant: Won't she feel threatened about this? You may not need a data processing manager anymore after you're up and running with the new system.

Mike: Really? We can save her salary? What do you suggest?

Consultant: We don't need her in the loop at this time, and it might behoove you not to tell her anything right now. I'll start searching out systems and software first and get the ball rolling. Let's set the next appointment date now to get together and review what I've found out, and then move forward from there.

Mike: Fine.

Proposals and the One-Call Sale

You must always remember that in very small to medium-size companies, only a relatively small percentage of buyers you will deal with are technical people, like accountants or engineers. A formal proposal will not be necessary most of the time.

Never Offer to Do a Proposal

More sales are lost by professional service providers who offer to do a proposal when one was unnecessary. This happens because they're too shy to secure a decision, or they simply don't know how to sell effectively. The only proposal you should ever do in this scenario is called an *engagement letter*.

Offering to do a proposal to a leader, socializer, executive, innovator, or overseer is sales-call suicide. The buyer's emotions will swing back to neutral or negative, and you both lose. The accountant/ engineer decision-maker, however, or one of the others, may occasionally want a proposal or "something in writing." In Chapter 12, we will discuss a painless approach—for you and the buyer—that enables you to close the sale and secure the client.

Now let's return to a situation where a proposal is requested:

Rose: Seymour, we're going to need to see something in writing.
Consultant: Okay. What specifically do you need to see in order for us to get started?
Rose: Well, I need to know exactly what services you will be providing, the fees, and the time frames for delivery of services.
Consultant: Let's set an appointment, then, for us to get together and review it in person.
Rose: Oh, that won't be necessary.
Consultant: No problem. Let's get together late this afternoon. I'll bring it by and we can review it.

The buyer must help write the proposal! She must tell you what she needs to see. Close the deal on a handshake, set the next appointment for as soon as possible, and stop off with the engagement letter on the way home before she changes her mind (a fact of life one has to deal with in sales is called buyer's remose). Get someone out there immediately to start reviewing the records and meeting their counterparts.

"Something in writing" has now been laid out for you by Rose. You would go back to your office, break out an engagement letter, give it to a secretary with Rose's modifications, and get it signed ASAP. I'll talk more about formal proposal writing in Chapter 12.

The One-Plus-One-Call Sale

Okay, you've tried to jockey for last position on what should be a one-call sale, and now you find out that the head honcho is talking to other firms. Or you just couldn't get in last.

The second best situation is to be first and last. Let's say you've had a great meeting with the owner or boss, but she had promised to talk to someone else. No great problem—if it's handled correctly! You must get a commitment from her that she will talk to you again before she makes a final decision, thus putting you last again. That conversation might sound like this:

Consultant: Maxine, what other information do you need for us to get started?
Buyer: I did promise to talk to my lawyer's computer consultant— gee, I forgot about that!

Consultant: Do you know this person?

Buyer: No, but she did come highly recommended.

Consultant: Fine. When are you supposed to meet with her?

Buyer: I haven't even spoken to her yet. I'll have to get her in here for an appointment.

Consultant: Is it necessary that you meet with her?

Buyer: Yes; my attorney requested it.

Consultant: When do you think you two might meet?

Buyer: As soon as she can make it!

Consultant: I have a favor to ask. I hope that you've found our meeting as productive as I have. I think we have a good match, and I'd like to work with you. I'm glad that your banker saw that possibility and referred me to you.

   I'd like to talk with you right *after* you've had a chance to meet with your attorney's computer consultant, but *before* you make a final decision on who you're going to use, in case anything comes up in her interview that we haven't discussed. Is that okay with you?

Buyer: I think there's a good match, too. Sure, we can do that.

Consultant: When should I call you to find out how your meeting went?

Buyer: I don't even have the appointment set, yet. I'll give you a call right after we meet.

This is not good. You must contact her—she may wait so long to meet with the other consultant that she forgets about you! Doubtful? What did you eat last night for dinner? How about a week ago Tuesday?

Consultant: How about if I give you a call Friday morning? Will you be around? In the meantime, I can meet again with your controller and her staff, review your records and systems, get to know their procedures better, and be prepared to move forward.

   If you happen to meet with her before then, you can give me a call. At this point, do you see any reason we won't be working together?

Buyer: That's fine with me. I do respect our attorney, but this woman is a total stranger. No, I don't know what should stop us from moving forward. I'll talk to you on Friday.

Consultant: Thanks.

While the prospective client waits to meet with the other consultant, you need to have as much contact with the business as possible.

Proceed as you normally would with a new client. Interview the staff. Take the controller out to lunch, and find out more about her aches. Meet the accounts receivable clerk and anyone else you'll be working with. Bring out any junior staff people who will be working with the client. Infect their premises so they start seeing you as their consultant now. Follow up your meeting with the buyer by sending a brochure and personal note at once. Keep your eyes open for an article to send immediately. You must maintain strong personal contact and control until after the engagement letter is signed.

Now, Friday morning rolls around and you're on the phone:

Consultant: Maxine, it's Jeff. How are you?
Buyer: Jeff! How are you?
Consultant: Super. What's going on?
Buyer: I set an appointment with my lawyer's consultant for next Thursday afternoon.
Consultant: Good. By the way, what's her name?
Buyer: Roberta Hoffman. Do you know her?
Consultant: Can't say that I do. Can I give you a call around five o'clock on Thursday? Do you think you'll be done by then?
Buyer: Sure, and thanks for the article.

Now you have some reconnaissance to do. Go back to your office and talk to your co-workers or other buddies or clients or other professionals. Find out what you can about your competition. Is she expensive? Cheap? What's her reputation for work product? Expertise in the buyer's industry and systems? You must be armed with information you can relate casually to your future client if the need arises (without deriding the competitor, of course). Also, you should have at least one contact with the client's business between now and your rival's appointment.

It's 4:59 P.M., Thursday afternoon, and you call Maxine.

Consultant: Hi. May I speak to Maxine please?
Receptionist: Sorry, she's left for the day. Would you like to leave a message?
Consultant: Yes. Please tell her that Jeff Feeshman called and that I'll call her tomorrow morning.

Darn! You told her you'd call and she's not in! What if she hired that other person? Oh, no! You may have failed!

Forget it. Blow it off. Get back to work immediately. The way to stay sane and sell more business is never to dwell on what may or may not happen. You must divert your attention immediately, and promise yourself you won't lose one minute's sleep over it. At this point, you have no indication whatsoever that she has hired the other consultant, except your own imagination. She may have had a problem at home or another appointment outside the office. Put a note in your calendar to call her first thing in the morning, and put it out of your mind. Life is too short to worry over what might happen without knowing the whole story.

The sales examination isn't complete yet; how can you issue a prognosis?

It's 9:00 A.M. on Friday morning:

Consultant: Maxine, hi. It's Jeff.
Buyer: Jeff, how are you?
Consultant: Okay. How did your appointment go with Ms. Hoffman?
Buyer: Fine. She's a real sweet person.
Consultant: And . . . ?
Buyer: And she seems like she knows what she's doing. She's worked with some of our attorney's clients for years.
Consultant: Where are you in the selection process?
Buyer: Actually, I'm leaning towards her right now.
Consultant: Really? How about sitting down one more time to discuss what we've seen in your records and systems and about your people that could be very important. You set the next appointment with her?
Buyer: No, I didn't. I told her I'd call her.
Consultant: What's your availability today? Lunch?
Buyer: No, I'm tied up all day. Monday is clear, though.
Consultant: Monday for lunch?
Buyer: Sure.
Consultant: See you then.

Once again, you need to put this situation out of your mind immediately. You will prepare a written agenda for Monday's lunch, showing how thorough you are. After that, forget it. Don't ruin your weekend, your time alone or with family, your chance to have fun.

Monday at lunch:

Consultant: I'm glad we could sit down and discuss the results of our inquiry.

Buyer: Go ahead.

Consultant: Your controller is a very nice person, but, because your business has grown and changed over the last five years, she is now approaching her professional capacity in terms of using up-to-date systems to run your company most efficiently.

Buyer: Do you recommend replacing her?

Consultant: Not at all. She's highly committted to the company and loyal to you. She just needs more guidance from your computer consultants. How much time did Roberta spend with Susie?

Buyer: None.

Consultant: I see. Susie and I and our manager on the job are going to have to communicate regularly. Did Roberta bring her staff people with her?

Buyer: No. She's self-employed but has other consultants who can assist her.

Consultant: And these people work with her all of the time, on every project and client?

Buyer: I doubt it. She pushed how much money she'd be saving us.

Consultant: Gee, I could've sworn you said that fees weren't your primary consideration. And not having the expertise you wanted around on your premises was one reason you were canning your old consultants.

Buyer: That's true. We need to have proactivity. We need to have people keep their eyes open for us to avoid some of the problems we've run into in the past.

Consultant: So Roberta won't be doing all the work herself. She'll have outsiders on your premises who don't work directly for her company and will be dealing with a well-meaning controller who needs professional guidance? Plus, she hasn't looked at your systems yet or interviewed your people? Did you talk to Susie about our meetings?

Buyer: Yes. Susie sought me out. She really likes you and wants to work with you.

Consultant: Where do we go from here?

Buyer: Let's go back to the office and get started.

Using Brochures in a Presentation

Sometimes, professional service providers think that people buy from brochures and that their presentation should be centered around their brochure.

This is false. A brochure is best used as a leave-behind piece or sent after an interview to make another contact with the prospective client, along with a hand-written thank-you note.

The real reason for having a brochure is that everyone else has one and you don't want to look unprofessional. I've been asked if it is important for sole proprietors to have a brochure. Well, it can enhance your credibility—but only if it looks right. Always remember, however, people buy other people.

Let's face it: Most brochures from professional service-providers look and read pretty much alike. The fancy ones have pictures of professionals (supposedly) working and their offices. They all say pretty much the same things: "We're great!" "We'll be your business partner!" "We're proactive!" "We're responsive!" Blah, blah, blah. . . .

Do you think buyers make decisions for professional services based on brochures? Leave your brochures at home on a sales interview.

Diagnosis and Rx: Do Only Presentations or Proposals That Will Nourish the Sale

- You will want to carefully manage the proposal and presentation process in order to facilitate your sale. Such careful planning will allow you to do as little work as possible and still get the business; satisfy the buyers' intellectual needs; give the buyer the opportunity to ask you questions; avoid wasting time and effort and giving away free ideas; give a custom-designed presentation or proposal (when necessary) that the buyer wants to see; and refrain from talking yourself out of a sale.
- Most small to medium-size companies will require only an informal presentation (as opposed to larger companies, which often go through an exhaustive formalized process to make a decision). An informal presentation should take a relatively short period of time; after the presentation, you should expect to leave with the business.
- After you've gone through the other steps in the sales examination (you've achieved good chemistry and found hurts, money, a commitment to action, and the decision-making process), you are ready to satisfy the buyers' intellectual needs by inviting them to ask you questions. These questions will form the basis of your informal presentation.
- Be careful in this step because there are only two possible reac-

tions to everything you say or propose: the buyer will either like it or dislike it. In order to avoid talking yourself out of a sale, remember:

1. Who you are talking to and what you are talking about. How your presentation is structured will depend on the buyer's personality type; the information you present will be based on the buyer's questions and your detailed notes.

Personality Type	Focus of Presentation
Leader	Results, not details
Executive/Manager	Security, buyer's benefits
Overseer	Welfare of the group
Socializer	Relationship aspects
Innovator	Freedom from mundane work
Accountant/Engineer	Value, details, credibility

   Also, with each type of buyer, you relate whatever you say to where they hurt and how you would ease their aches.

2. Get to the point; don't ramble on.
3. Tell the buyer stories (brief case histories) that back up your claims.
4. Don't make claims you can't support.
5. Don't answer unasked questions unless you know for a fact that the client must hear about it. If you ever hear the words, "Oh, by the way . . ." coming out of your mouth, you are in deep trouble; everything you say can and will be held against you.

▸ Do not center your presentation around your brochure; leave it at home on a sales interview. People do not buy professional services based on brochures; they buy based on the appearance and demeanor of the seller.
▸ In small to medium-size companies, only a relatively small percentage of buyers will be accountant/engineer types; therefore, a formal proposal will not be necessary most of the time.
▸ Never offer to do a proposal. For leaders, socializers, executives, innovators, and overseers, the only proposal you should ever do is an engagement letter. Offering to do a proposal for any of these leaders is sales suicide.

11

Take Two Aspirins,
But I'll Call You
In the Morning

In this chapter, you'll discover more about presentations for small to medium-size firms. Here you'll learn how to handle the two-call sale, those situations where you have to come back and meet with the real decision-makers, versus the one-call sale where you have the decision-makers in front of you and they are ready to go. And we will review the two-plus-one sale where you have to jockey for last position over your competitors.

In Step 5, you tested everything you could about the buyers' decision-making process, and you used these tests to ascertain whether you could influence that procedure to your benefit. This chapter will guide you through the ticklish—and sometimes hazardous—presentation and proposal process and help you to be more successful at it for the two-call sale. This is step 7: Prepare a Custom-Designed Presentation and/or Proposal.

A Brief Review

To quickly review from Chapter 10, you should test the presentation and proposal process in order to:

1. Do as little work as possible and still get the business.
2. Satisfy the buyers' intellectual needs.
3. Give the buyers the opportunity to ask you questions.
4. Avoid wasting time, effort, and giving away free ideas.

5. Give a custom-designed presentation or proposal (if necessary) that the buyer wants to hear.
6. Avoid talking yourself out of a sale.

Let's review where you are in the two-call sale:

- You and the prospective client have been developing a comfortability and chemistry with each other.
- The client is telling you his emotional needs, wants, desires, and musts, as well as the background information necessary for you to diagnose the situation.
- The buyer is committed to action.
- You are comfortable with the buyer's willingness to pay your fees.
- You have acquired a mentor who is guiding you through the sale to a successful result.
- You found out what the decision-making process is and have determined your ability to influence the process.
- You've eliminated as much of your competition as possible.
- You've jockeyed for last position.
- Your next appointment is set with the final decision-maker(s).

Now, you need to address the presentation process. If you have conducted the sales examination correctly, your closing ratio should be approximately 90 percent from this point forward.

The Two-Call Sales Presentation

In the sales examination Step 5, you secured a coach and learned who the decision-makers are and what they want to see or hear in order for you to get hired.

In order to maintain continuity of thought and discovery of the sales examination process, let's backtrack a little to the buying scenario with Bernie, the CPA, from Chapter 9. In that chapter Bernie questioned Bob, one of the buyers, in order to discover the decision-making process for assigning the audit. Bob responded that his company was considering seven CPA firms. Bob's job was to narrow the field down to three firms, and present those firms to Ms. Jones for final selection.

Bernie continued to interview Bob about the selection process, asking him detailed questions about how the process was going so far, what firms were being considered, and what Bob liked and disliked about these firms. He also asked what Ms. Jones would be most interested in seeing and hearing, so he would know how to structure his final presentation.

During the course of this discussion, Bernie questioned Bob as to who else might have influence over the final decision. Bob mentioned the firm's attorney, Jane Doe, and banker, Nate Rate. Bernie made plans to talk to both of them.

On Friday, after Bob met with the other firms, Bernie called to find out how these meetings went. He systematically and delicately questioned Bob regarding what he liked and disliked about each firm, thereby narrowing the field down to a couple of competitors. Bernie also made arrangements to be the last firm to make a presentation to Ms. Jones.

We pick up the process on Tuesday, when Bernie calls Bob to confirm his presentation appointment:

Bob: Bob speaking.
Bernie: Bob, it's Bernie. How are you doing?
Bob: Okay. You're scheduled for Friday afternoon at three o'clock.
Bernie: What about the other two firms?
Bob: They're coming in Thursday afternoon and Friday morning.
Bernie: Thanks. In order for me to be best prepared, can we sit down this afternoon or Wednesday to look at your books and further discuss Ms. Jones's goals? I'd also like to meet more of your people.
Bob: Is that necessary? I'm tied up this afternoon and Wednesday is real tight.
Bernie: In my experience it pays to be more prepared than less for meetings like this. I want to make sure we hit all the right issues for you and Ms. Jones. What's convenient for you?
Bob: I can bring you in at eight on Thursday morning, which is about two hours before the first firm shows up.
Bernie: That would be fine. See you then.

Bernie's in a time crunch himself. He had appointments scheduled for Thursday and had hoped to be finished preparing for the meeting with Bob and Ms. Jones by Wednesday night. He will now rearrange his appointments, because he knows this is an opportunity to secure an important new client with his odds of success being very high.

In the meantime, before Thursday's appointment, Bernie will review his detailed notes and begin preparing for Friday's meeting. He will review the aches described by Bob in the initial interview and Bob's conditions of satisfaction. He will reference his memory banks and sales files on the clients he's acquired and be prepared to relate Bob's situation to a concrete third-party example of a circumstance he, or someone else in the firm, has handled successfully before. If he doesn't have any direct experience with this sort of situation, he'll ask around the firm for someone who does and debrief them fully or invite them to come with him.

On Thursday morning he'll select the audit manager who will accompany him to the interview on Friday. This isn't a formal presentation and the company doesn't appear to have any major tax issues. If they did, he would bring along a tax partner or manager. Although Bernie wants to be prepared, he is cautious about bringing too many people on this interview. Bernie will set an agenda for Thursday's preliminary meeting with Bob.

On Friday Bernie will be prepared with specific solutions to Bob's concerns and armed with references to third-party case studies that he will present verbally or distribute in written form (if necessary). He has called and spoken to Jane Doe, the attorney. Although he was not able to meet with her personally, he's gotten to know her and has learned more about the client's situation through their conversations. He did have breakfast Monday morning with Nate Rate, the banker. Rate told him that Bob's company is a valued bank customer with ever-increasing capital needs in a quickly changing industry.

Let's attend a portion of Thursday's meeting:

Bernie: Thanks for giving me an opportunity to meet with you this morning. I'd like to introduce Audrey, one of our audit managers. She is one of the finest people we have and has experience with many of our clients in your industry. Can we take a look at the financials, general ledger, disbursement and receipts journals, and the tax returns?

Bob: Sure. I'll introduce you to Mary, our accounting manager. She can get you the information you need.

Bernie and Audrey meet with the accounting manager and listen to her concerns and hurts as well. They discover additional information about the relationship with the current accountant that Bob wasn't aware of, such as the constant training time staff has been forced to spend with the myriad of people rotating through their office from the current CPA firm. Audrey has begun the process of developing a relationship with Mary.

Based on the records and review of the invoices from the current CPA firm, Bernie starts nailing down estimated fees for Ms. Jones and Bob. He reviews the tax return and prepares a list of questions he will review with Bob about possibilities for tax savings for the client.

Bernie and Audrey make a point of being introduced to everyone in the office. Audrey makes a point of spending some time alone with Mary, her counterpart on the audit. They meet again with Bob before they leave:

Bernie: Thanks for letting us meet with Mary.

Audrey: She seems quite dedicated.

Bob: Oh, she is. Ms. Jones really likes her.

Bernie: Is there anything that has come up since we last met that we should be prepared for?

Bob: Not really.

Bernie: Audrey, I need to talk about something with Bob in private.

Audrey: Okay. [*She leaves.*]

Bernie: Bob, I have two favors to ask. Number one, sometimes people get tired of the interview process and cut it short. It's happened to me once before. Is it possible that Ms. Jones might make a decision before meeting with us tomorrow?

Bob: No, she's looking forward to meeting with you.

Bernie: Great! The other request is that you talk to Mary and see how she and Audrey hit it off. That's a vital relationship, and I want to make sure we have the best match. If there's a problem, please let me know right away.

Bob: Makes sense. I'll talk to her as soon as you leave.

Bernie: Thanks. Where will the meeting be held?

Bob: In our conference room.

Bernie: Good. We'll see you Friday afternoon at three o'clock. Please let me know if anything else comes up that I should know about.

Bernie and Audrey leave their future client and debrief immediately once they get to the car. They continue their conversation in a conference room at their office. They each review the client's aches from Bob's standpoint and from Mary's to make sure they don't miss anything. They put together an agenda of tomorrow's meeting in order to gain control of the meeting; to be professional, organized, and prepared; and to be very different from their competitors who will be *selling* their firms. Bernie knows that Bob and Ms. Jone will be buying *people*, not firms.

Bernie will not bring anyone else to the meeting besides Audrey (unless he hears back from Bob). There aren't any burning tax or other technical issues to discuss. Although this client would be a nice gem to add to the family jewels, Bernie doesn't want to overwhelm Bob and Ms. Jones. The meeting must be kept casual and open in order for there to be a free flow of information and feelings.

The second (and hopefully final) meeting on a two-call sale (with Bob and Ms. Jones) must cover the following issues to be most effective.

1. *Chemistry.* The sales process starts all over again with Ms. Jones. Because Bernie has done a good job of creating chemistry with Bob (the user decision-maker) and Audrey has started a relationship with Mary (a user decision-maker influencer), he is ahead of his competitors in completing the circle of comfortability with Ms. Jones (the money woman). This is akin to being introduced to a friend of a friend.

To ensure that good chemistry is created during Friday's meeting, Bernie will control to the best of his ability the location of the meeting, the physical and psychological well-being of his prospective clients, and the meeting itself.

2. *Where It Hurts.* Bernie and Audrey know where it hurts for Bob and Mary. These aches need to be reviewed, since pain tends to go away and Ms. Jones may not be aware of their hurts.

Ms. Jones' aches need to be introduced and diagnosed at this meeting, too; hers may be significantly different from the others. And Bernie must also diagnose whether Ms. Jones is committed to change.

3. *Their Conditions of Satisfaction.* Bernie must uncover what it will take to make sure Ms. Jones and Bob are delighted clients, and he must negotiate from there. This continues the client relationship management process Bernie has already begun.

Chances are superb that Bernie's competitors won't ask for the buyers' conditions of satisfaction, which will create a huge and powerful distinction between him and them. Even if they did, Bernie can smoke out what the buyers told his rivals, expand upon it, and negotiate from there—as well as subtly induce holes in any unlikely service claims made by another firm.

4. *Fees.* The fee issues need to be raised again; Ms. Jones may have different goals from Bob's.

5. *The Decision-Making Process.* Bernie needs to find out from Ms. Jones exactly what her decision-making strategy is. He will discuss the other people who have influence and are involved in the process, and will try to deliver a knockout punch to his rivals.

6. *A Presentation the Buyers Want to See.* Bernie is armed with similar successfully resolved situations and referral sources. New Issues may arise, which is why an informal presentation will work best here; this is not a dog and pony show. Bernie will find out in the meeting what the buyers need to see and hear in order for him to get the work, and he will alter his presentation accordingly.

7. *Closure.* Bernie has jockeyed for last position in order to leave with the business today. He knows that the buyers are most likely to want to end the selection process and get back to producing results for their company.

He is not afraid of securing a decision at this meeting because he knows the risks of not doing so: the buyers could cool off, a rival might weasel his way back in, the buyers could get involved in an emergency situation and everything would be tabled, or the decision could be postponed and a painful fee-negotiation process begun.

Sound like a lot of work? A thorough examination always is. Conduct the same high-quality due diligence on a sales examination as you do on any of your work projects, and you will be able to issue a clean bill of success!

Successful Team Selling

Bernie and Audrey will be entering a team selling situation. In some ways it is much more powerful to sell with someone else than alone. In other ways the situation is much more complicated and if the members of the team don't know their roles, they could end up stepping all over each other and causing confusion.

The Advantage of Team Selling

There are several vital advantages to working as a team when attempting to bring in a new client or to sell additional business to an existing client. Team selling:

- *Provides Psychological Support.* Don't laugh—this is the most important factor in favor of going in as a team. It's a lot easier for those who are quite risk-averse to approach the selling situation in tandem, rather than alone. It eases the fear of the unknown and the fear of potential rejection. There is less chance of feeling overwhelmed or double/triple-teamed in the sales interview. Working as a team also allows one to share and compound the joy of victory with a comrade in arms, and ease the defeat by shouldering it with someone else.

- *Increases Available Knowledge.* "Two heads are better than one." Having two people on a sales call increases the chances of asking the important questions that need to be asked to elicit the prospective client's needs.
- *Serves as Learning Opportunity.* Team selling allows the members to rehash the sales interview afterward to discover what worked and didn't work for future reference.
- *Introduces the Players.* Bringing key people who would interact with the prospective client can be a powerful sales tool. If the client likes the people they will be working with, a good portion of the sale is already made.
- *Increases Available Expertise.* By having the right team members on the sales call, questions raised by the prospective client can be answered intelligently by experts.

The Dangers of Team Selling

To avoid losing business, one must be aware of the hazards of team selling that can overshadow the advantages and result in lost sales and bad impressions:

- *Confusion.* How do you think prosective clients feel when they see professionals stepping over each other's sentences? Ever have your partner contradict you in front of a client? Professionals must be perceived as effective and organized. A confusing sales call always leads to lost business opportunities.
- *Overwhelming the prospect.* Pretend you're a buyer of professional services. How would you feel if a firm showed up with nineteen people on a sales call? Don't laugh, it's a true story. Very often professionals think the more, the merrier applies to selling. Wrong! Don't do anything to create fear or overwhelm the buyers' side of the table.

The Ten Rules of Effective Team Selling

In order to work effectively and create the desired result, certain guidelines of team selling need to be followed:

Rule 1: Select Team Members Carefully. Make sure there is a good chemistry among those going on the sales call. Don't bring people that don't like each other; this lack of chemistry is unspoken but is always perceived by the prospective client.

Rule 2: There Must Be an "Orchestrator." Someone should be the lead person on the interview. This person maintains order and control in the meeting, asks the majority of the questions, and directs the clients' inquiries to the proper person for the best possible answers.

Rule 3: Stage a "Pre-Briefing." There always must be a pre-meeting briefing to discuss the agenda for the meeting and to develop the correct plan of action.

Rule 4: Prepare Questions. All team members should prepare three questions that are brought to the pre-briefing. At that time, the most vital questions can be sorted into the agenda.

Rule 5: Keep It to a Minimum. Only bring those players that are absolutely necessary. Remember "Malthus's Rule of Team Selling": As one increases the number of people on a sales call arithmetically, the potential for problems increases geometrically!

Rule 6: Answer Questions Succinctly. All too often, sales interviews involving teams turn into "educational seminars" that can not only bore the prospective clients silly but also fail to allow enough time for you to get important concerns answered by the buyers.

Rule 7: Be Flexible as to Your Agenda. You may think the meeting should go one way, but the client has another agenda in mind. Be flexible enough to allow them to get their needs met, and they will feel better about you as a possible provider of services.

Rule 8: Team Members Must Be on the Same Wavelength. Make sure everyone involved knows not to contradict other team members or to step on their sentences. There must also be enough "space" for the client to air their concerns. Everyone must share the same goals going into the meeting.

Rule 9: Sell Something! Be committed to selling some piece of business every time you go out as a team, even if it is a small study about a potential problem. Make your in-

vestment of time and effort pay off by getting your foot
in the door somehow.

Rule 10: Hold a Debriefing. Discuss what worked and didn't
work, as well as the appropriate follow-up by selected
team members.

The Final Presentation

Let's go on an abbreviated version of the sales presentation with Bernie and Audrey. Your presentations in similar situations in the past may not resemble what you are about to observe. However, if you have conducted your sales examination correctly, nine out of ten sales calls in this situation will be very much like this one.

This is an informal presentation versus a full-blown dog and pony show; those will be discussed in Chapter 12.

The purpose of this presentation is to:

- Create an open and friendly environment to promote a lot of input from the buyers.
- Find out the money woman's aches.
- Qualify her for fees.
- Cover the decision-making process.
- Present what they need to know and want to hear.
- Close the business and leave with a new client.
- Block any comeback possibilities by their current accountants or your other rivals.

2:35 P.M.—Bernie and Audrey meet in the lobby. They pre-brief about the appointment. They have decided that Bernie will orchestrate, but Audrey must take a dynamic role—without each stepping on the other's words. Bernie has expressed his confidence in her and assures her that the outcome will be what they want to happen.

2:50 P.M.—Bernie and Audrey arrive, announce themselves to the receptionist, and have a seat in the foyer. Audrey is nervous; this is only her third such sales call. Bernie is nervous, too; however, because of his experience in bringing in business, he realizes that his nervousness is absolutely normal and to be expected. So, instead of fighting the fear, he accepts it, and it dissipates. Because he has conducted a good sales examination, he also knows that his closing percentage in situations like this is about 90 percent.

3:04 P.M.—Young and Olde are leaving the conference room

where the presentations are being held. There are five of them and they are slapping themselves on the back and congratulating themselves on a job well done. Bernie feels sick to his stomach.

Bob (Bernie's coach and the user decision-maker) greets them in the lobby. They exchange pleasantries.

Bernie: Looks like Young and Olde did a great job in there. Should we even bother to do our presentation?

Bob: They were okay. I strongly suggest you and Audrey talk to Ms. Jones. Come on and I'll introduce you to her.

3:12 P.M.—Greetings and introductions are made. Bob and Audrey take out note pads.

Bernie: Thanks for meeting with us. What would you two like to make sure we accomplish in this meeting?

Jones: I need to find out how you are going to help me to better run my business. Bob has spoken nicely about you, but his area is finance and accounting. I'm in a tough, competitive business and need business advice.

Bernie: Good. Anything else?

Jones: Of course we need to discuss fees and your previous experience in our industry.

Bernie: Bob?

Bob: I agree with Ms. Jones. But I think she also needs to hear how you're going to keep disruptions to a minimum.

Bernie: Fine. We've prepared an agenda that I believe will answer your concerns. [*Bernie passes out copies of the agenda.*] I always like to begin engagements by finding out how my clients will be kept satisfied. We've built our practice with delighted clients and their referrals, and the best way that I've found is to find out up-front what the client needs to see after they've started using us.

How would you know that you had made the right decision by hiring us? What evidence could we look back at six months from now and have you be able to say that you were satisfied?

Bob: We have to get this audit completed and have the financials to the bank no later than eight weeks after the fiscal year-end. And Mary and I can't constantly be bothered with questions.

Bernie: I know we've talked about some of this before, but what's been your experience so far with your current accountant?

Bob: He makes promises he can't keep. They've finished the audit a month late every year for the last three years. The bank gets anxious and hassles me. And I wind up spending my time training his people to audit our company because the people he puts on the job rotate so frequently and are inexperienced.

Bernie: Has this affected you in any way, Ms. Jones? Isn't Nate Rate your banker over at Frank National? I've worked with Nate for years.

Jones: Why yes, he is. Banks are so much more uptight than they were only a few years ago. Everyone's scared of the regulators and their auditors, too! Because our business is capital-intensive, we've always had to finance our equipment purchases to stay state-of-the-art. The longer they wait to get the financial statements, the more they talk about boosting their rate, and the more time it takes to approve our loans. I don't want to pay one cent more than I should have to in order to borrow money.

Also, Bob hasn't been able to do as many of my special projects as I'd like. Are you going to be able to finish the audit on time?

Bernie: I wouldn't be sitting here if I didn't think we could do the job. We need delighted clients like you to refer us to their friends who might be in a similar circumstance.

Okay, what other conditions of satisfaction do you have?

Jones: I need people to bring me ideas on how to better run my business. I would think that with as many clients as a CPA firm has, you would run across ideas to save money that we might implement to create better results. We wouldn't mind some help with strategic planning. CPAs seem to be historians—they only tell you what's wrong after it's happened instead of helping prevent it.

Bob: Every year we pay more federal and state taxes, but no one comes to me with any ideas on how to cut that down before the fact. Also, I've got to have my questions answered and calls returned faster.

Bernie: What's happening now?

Bob: Sometimes it takes two days to get back to me. The person I've been dealing with has basically kissed me off and turned me over to someone else. No offense, Audrey, but I need to deal at the partner level sometimes.

Jones: Our fees have been very much out of line with the marketplace. We need to cut costs.

Bernie: This is a good time to discuss fees. First let us recap what you've said your conditions of satisfaction would be: You said that you need to get the audit finished and have the financials to the bank no later than eight weeks after the fiscal year-end. You want us to keep our promises so you can improve your banking relationship, which directly effects how you run your company.

Bob, you and Mary can't constantly be bothered with questions from inexperienced staff auditors. Bob would like less staff rotation.

Ms. Jones, you said you'd be satisfied if we brought ideas to you on a regular basis to help you better manage your business. You also mentioned a strategic planning role, and Bob mentioned he wants tax advice before you have to pay.

Bob wants better response time and more interaction with the partner on the job. Ms. Jones wants to cut fees.

Let me ask this, how often should the three or four of us be sitting down to discuss your business, even outside of the audit? Would a quarterly review be in order? We could review what's happened over the previous quarter and discuss the next quarter.

Jones: That would be very good.

Bernie: Did I miss any points regarding how you'd be satisfied?

Jones: I don't think so.

Bernie: All right. Now's a good time to get fees out of the way. Is that okay with you?

Jones: Yes.

Bernie: I know we've discussed this, but sometimes people keep their existing service providers after all. Have you made a firm decision not to keep your current accountant, or is it possible he will be retained?

Bob: It's possible; Joe Blow has been our accountant for years and is one of the three finalists.

Bernie: I see. So it's quite likely that you'll keep Joe after all?

Jones: I really like him.

Bernie: You're right about the marketplace for CPA services. Some firms in this area are offering dramatic fee incentives to obtain new clients and keep their old ones. Last year, you paid your acocuntant about $18,000. Have you been quoted lower fees by the others you're talking to?

Bob: Yes. One firm offered to do it for $9,500.

Bernie: Amazing! Have you then decided to go with the cheapest firm?

Jones: Not necessarily.

Bernie: As I discussed earlier with Bob, we're usually not the cheapest firm, and most likely we won't be any less expensive than your current firm. We absolutely won't cut corners to get any engagement. Our goal is not to wind up in court as defendants in a negligence suit because we took a client in that we couldn't afford to service properly. We also believe that we should make a fair profit.

If you are looking for the cheapest accountants, you can find there are probably others out there who will take that risk. Audrey, why don't you explian to Ms. Jones about the situation we ran into last year over in Bushtown?

Audrey: Sure. Ms. Jones, I don't think we do the client any favor by doing what could be an incomplete or a hit-or-miss job. Our job is not only to verify whether your financial statements fairly represent the financial status of your company. There are certain concerns that will usually turn up in an audit--if the people are properly trained to look and listen for them—that the client may not be aware of. We look at an audit as a way of coming to the client with ideas on how to improve their business in many different areas.

Last year, Bernie and I came across a situation in a slightly larger company that we brought in as a new client. The company had hired a firm whose fees were approximately two-thirds of their previous CPA's! This company saw auditing services as generic and had been promised the moon by the new firm.

Sometimes people get what they pay for. Because the fees were so low, the accountants assigned very inexperienced people who were improperly managed, and the effect was to delay the audit by six weeks longer than it was before. In this economy, the bankers got nervous and the shareholders and board weren't too pleased, either.

Because the accounting firm was so rushed to get the work out, the numbers were wrong and the financial statements were not only late but had to be rescinded and then reissued. Unfortunately, the person that thought she was doing her best by hiring the cheapest firm caught the heat on that one. The CPA firm was fired immediately and we got a new client.

Frankly, I can't understand why companies insist on saving a relatively minor amount of money off their bottom line. Although, at the time, the amount may seem like a lot of money dollar for dollar, it's not worth it if they wind up putting their business, shareholder, banking, and board of director relationships at risk. I know that $8,500 is a lot of money. For $7,000 in the situation over in Bushtown, they almost lost their new line of credit, their banking relationship, and a great interest rate they worked years to get.

Fortunately, my team was able to straighten out what had turned into a mess and get them the financials on time this past fiscal year. They asked us to sit down with the bankers and review the statements with them, and we did that. The bankers were satisfied and have referred some new clients to us since then. We'll do everything we can to leverage off your people to save you fees and speed up the process.

I think you'll find our people are better compensated than at many other firms because we want to keep the good ones and thus have less turnover for the client to deal with. We invest almost 5 percent of gross revenues in training our partners and staff to keep them up-to-date on what is a very changing profession and to be more efficient in their work.

What we will do is give you a heck of a lot more than just a traditional audit. I think strategic planning is definitely in order to start our relationship, so that we can find out exactly where you're going.

Bernie and I will sit down with you quarterly to review your business and make recommendations, as you've requested. Bob, you'll have more contact with Bernie, but you have to realize that I'll be your manager on the job.

Bernie: Audrey is really an expert at what she does, but I'll still be reviewing the progress of her audit team. What was Mary's feedback about her conversation with Audrey the other day?

Bob: Oh, Mary likes Audrey and feels comfortable with her.

Audrey: That's nice. She seems quite competent and she really cares about your company.

Bernie: That's good to hear. We'll also need the cooperation of all of your people to speed the audit up. I think we've covered fees; should we proceed?

Jones: Are you going to charge us extra for the strategic planning and meeting with us quarterly?

Bernie: No. We won't be charging you for the initial strategic planning meeting nor for the quarterly meetings which we usually conduct with the client over lunch. The strategic planning is worth at least $3,000 to $5,000 and the quarterly consultations are worth $500 to $1,000 each.

If you want us to get involved in a lengthy strategic planning process, we'll need to talk about a time investment and fees. In this case, I feel that Bob and his staff are absolutely capable of doing the detail work with our input and direction.

Our goal is to have healthy clients who pay our bills on time and refer us to their contacts and counterparts in other businesses. We see strategic planning and a quarterly review as our investment in you.

Audrey: Also, Mary will be freed up from some of the extra hours she has had to put in training and managing your existing accountant's audit staff. Did you know that she's had to take time away from her family by working Sundays during the audit these past three years, just to catch up on her own work because of the constant rotation of staff and retraining?

Jones: No, I wasn't aware of that.

Audrey: How have your conversations gone with the other firms you interviewed before us?

Bob: Young and Olde seems big enough to handle our account— they're the ones who offered to do our audit for $9,500. And, of course, good old Joe Blow is still in the running.

Audrey: What did you like about Young and Olde?

Jones: They're one of the largest firms in the city and a national firm who could help us in many different areas. They talked about a network of experts all over the U.S. who would be available to us at any time. They seemed very professional.

Audrey: Bob?

Bob: I'm not impressed. They hardly asked any questions and didn't spend any time with me or Mary to find out what we really needed, like you and Bernie did. Also, they have the reputation of buying audits so that they can stuff add-on services down the client's throat. Their partner is very impressive but wouldn't commit to spending any time with us.

Audrey: Where do you stand with Joe Blow?

Jones: Joe knows that he's had some problems in the past with staffing our audit. He's been our accountant forever. Of course, he's promised to correct any problems.

Bob: He says that every year.

Audrey: Is Joe set up to do strategic planning, computer consulting, cash management services, health care consulting, and other client-related assistance?

Jones: I don't know.

Bob: He's in over his head on our account.

Jones: What do you suggest, Bob?

Bob: We've outgrown Joe. I suggest we move on.

Jones: Can't we continue to use him somehow?

Bob: I can't see how.

Jones: Bernie, would we keep Joe involved?

Bernie: I respect how you feel. We go out of our way to develop this kind of loyalty you have with Joe with our clients, too. Sometimes companies simply outgrow their existing CPAs.

I'm sorry, but we don't work with other accounting firms unless we absolutely have to. For instance, we've worked with them in the past in a city new to us, and it makes sense to use them for an inventory observation. The problem is that I can't be responsible for Joe's quality of work.

Audrey: What other questions do you have for us?

Jones: Do you have other clients in our industry?

Bernie: Yes. We've been servicing clients in this business for over fifteen years. Actually, our firm has grown with clients like you, which started out small and have become big players in the industry, usually in the second generation of the business.

Because the needs of our clients have grown, we've had to expand our service offerings into nonaccounting areas such as computer selection and installation, health care consulting, inventory control management. You've done quite a job of growing your business, which was started by your father, right?

Jones: Yes. Dad retired eight years ago. Our sales have tripled since then.

But what about working for our competitors? I can't have them find out what we're doing. We're Joe's only client in this business.

Audrey: Please understand that we are bound by strong professional standards that we must maintain, and we have confidentiality agreements with our clients. We can't and won't endanger our relationships in any way by relating what's happening with one client to another. Nor will they have access to your records.

Because we have other clients in your industry, we've developed an expertise that will allow us to become familiar much faster with your operations and systems than someone else.

Bernie: Do you have any other questions?

Jones: No.

Bob: No.

Bernie: Can we set a date for the first strategic planning session?

Dates are set for an initial strategic planning session. Audrey will secure some records to review over the weekend and return them on

Monday. She will have an appointment with Ms. Jones on Monday to sign the engagement letter. Dates are set for Audrey's people to start some preliminary work immediately.

Bernie sets a lunch date with Ms. Jones to get to know her personal goals and her business better. Bernie and Audrey set a date with Bob and Mary to gain a more specific overview of their systems and records.

The conversation continues:

Bernie: What'll you think Joe will say when he finds out you've hired us? When do you plan on telling him?

Jones: He'll have a fit. We're his biggest client. I need to tell him right away.

Bernie: What do you think he'll do?

Bob: Oh, he'll beg, promise, and possibly even cry. We tried to change CPAs about six years ago and he wound up keeping the work.

Bernie: Ms. Jones, what do you think will happen?

Jones: Bob's right.

Bernie: Do you think you'll keep Joe again?

Bob: I don't see how we can. It's hurting me, my people, and our business.

Jones: Painful as it will be, we must go through with it.

Bernie: How can I help?

Jones: I'm not sure.

Bernie: We can make the transition as easy as possible, and there are times, of course, when we run into business that is simply too small for us to handle. After we get done reviewing Joe's records and meeting with him, if I like what I see, we might be able to start referring some small business to him as the need arises.

Jones: That would be nice.

Note: Some professional service providers carry blank engagement letters with them to be filled in and signed at once. The whole weekend looms ahead for Ms. Jones to change her mind—we will discuss the after-sale (avoiding back-outs) some more in Chapter 13.

5:02 P.M.—Bernie and Audrey leave with a new client. They quickly go to their car and begin reviewing what worked well and what didn't. Overall, they are delighted with the results. They make a commitment not to worry about the possibility of Ms. Jones changing her mind over the weekend.

You Can't Sell Higher Fees Unless You Believe That Your Firm And You Are Worth the Money

I know how tough the economy is in various parts of the country. Please remember: The top business producers in every profession are still selling business at good fees. In my consulting business, I have had the good fortune of interacting with many of them on a regular basis. This book is designed to teach you how not to cut fees and how to get the business you want.

Are you going to run into situations where people are going to buy strictly on fees? Sure, but you have to decide if you want these people as your clients. Can you service them capably? Are you shooting yourself in the foot by giving the business away today, hoping to increase fees in the future? What do you think will happen when you try to raise your fees in the future with a client who is only interested in the cheapest service provider? Do they also go to the cheapest dentist in town?

On the other hand, when selling fees, consider the buyer's opportunity and commitment to actively bring you referrals. That's one reason to accept an engagement for lower fees. Also, sometimes it's wise to buy a market; that is, to sell your services for a lower fee than normal in order to break into a new market, grab some market share, and then use your happy client as a source of referrals and third-party verifications as to the quality of your work.

Bernie chose not to cut fees in order to buy the business, but decided instead to include some value-added services, strategic planning and quarterly reviews, in order to maintain his fee structure. That was his choice; he was in control. He is also wise enough to know that the more interaction he has with a satisfied client, the more likely he is to get golden referrals and more business from that client. Bernie looks at this as marketing to his current clients.

The Two-Plus-One-Call Sales Presentation

Okay, you tried to be last and find out that you can't be. Let's backtrack a bit to Bernie's conversation with Bob before the presentation:

Bernie: Because new issues may arise in their meetings with you and Ms. Jones, I request that you set their appointments first. I would appreciate it very much if we could be last. When should I get back to you to find out when they're scheduled to come in?

Bob: Blow has already done that. We feel obligated to meet with him last because he's been with us so long.

Now Bernie would have trouble. Joe Blow is going to plead, cry, and beg not to lose his best client. That sometimes works! Bernie needs to do one heck of a job in the presentation step to make sure Blow doesn't keep this client.

Bernie: How does Ms. Jones feel about that?
Bob: I don't know. But she's fond of old Joe.

Look out below. Bernie's prepared, though. He'll just have to jockey for last once more when he gets to the presentation step. Let's return to Bernie and Audrey's meeting with Bob and Ms. Jones:

Bernie: Do you have any other questions?
Jones: No.
Bob: No.
Bernie: Can we set a date for the first strategic planning session?
Jones: I've promised to meet with Joe before we make any final decision. I owe him that much.
Audrey: Can we set some tentative dates then? That way I can have my calendar clear in case you decide to move forward.
Jones: That makes sense.
Bernie: What do you think Joe will say when he finds out you're planning on working with us? When do you plan on meeting with him?
Jones: He'll have a fit. We're his biggest client. I need to tell him right away.
Bernie: What do you think he'll do?
Bob: Oh, he'll beg, promise, and possibly even cry. We tried to change CPAs about six years ago and he wound up keeping the work.
Bernie: Ms. Jones, what do you think will happen?
Jones: Bob's right.
Bernie: Do you think you'll keep Joe again?
Bob: I don't see how we can. It's hurting me, my people, and our business.
Jones: Painful as it will be, we must go through with it.
Bernie: How can I help?
Jones: I'm not sure.
Bernie: We can make the transition as easy as possible and there are

times, of course, when we run into business that is simply too small for us to handle. After we get done reviewing Joe's records and meeting with him, if I like what I see, we might be able to start referring some small business to him as the need arises.

Jones: That would be nice.

Bernie: Here's my experience in similar situations. Right now you see a need to trade up to a bigger firm who will give you better all-around service. Joe's not going to let this go under any circumstances. Old relationships are very hard to break.

Before you say no, I suggest you turn Joe's next appointment into a transition meeting. I'll stop by with an engagement letter Monday morning on the way in to work. I hope I'm not being too forward, but this is an emotional issue that must be dealt with directly. If you have engaged us, there's not much Joe can do.

Jones: I don't know . . .

Bob: I do. We must make a change. We need Bernie and Audrey's firm, or we're holding back our business and hurting our employees, like Mary and me.

Jones: All right.

You still haven't secured that client, but you're in a much better position than if you don't get the engagement letter signed. If they're really committed to change, they'll do it. See Chapter 10 for the One-Plus-One-Call Sale to see how to handle that.

What You've Accomplished In Steps 6 and 7

You've satisfied the reasons for testing the proposal and presentation process:

1. You've done the work necessary (and not any extra) to get the business.
2. You've satisfied the buyers' intellectual needs.
3. You gave the buyers the opportunity to ask you questions.
4. You avoided wasting time and effort and giving away free ideas.
5. You conducted a custom-designed presentation or proposal (if necessary) that the buyers wanted to see or hear.
6. You didn't talk yourself out of a sale.

How to Proceed in the Sales Interview
After the Presentation in a Two-Call Sale

In Step 6, you tested to see if a presentation or a proposal was necessary, and you found out what a proposal would look like. In Step 7, you conducted a presentation or wrote a proposal that the buyers wanted to see. Now you need to proceed immediately to Step 8 and the formalization of the agreement—closure.

Diagnosis and Rx: Do Only Presentations or Proposals That Will Nourish the Sale *and* Whenever You've Got a New Patient in Front of You, Be Sure to Give Them a Thorough Examination

▸ You will want to carefully manage the proposal and presentation process in order to facilitate your sale. Such careful planning will allow you to do as little work as possible and still get the business; satisfy the buyers' intellectual needs; give the buyer the opportunity to ask you questions; avoid wasting time and effort and giving away free ideas; give a custom-designed presentation or proposal (when necessary) that the buyer wants to see; and refrain from talking yourself out of a sale.

▸ If, during the course of the sales examination, you meet with a new patient (decision-maker) along the way, you must give that individual a complete examination. This examination must include chemistry, where it hurts, conditions of satisfaction, fees, the decision-making process, a presentation (when required), and closure.

▸ Team selling has several advantages, including the following:

1. Provides psychological support. It's easier to approach a selling situation with someone else.
2. Increases available knowledge. "Two heads are better than one."
3. Serves as a learning opportunity. After the sales call, you can rehash what worked and what didn't for future reference.
4. Introduces the players. Team selling enables the prospect to meet key people who will be working on the job if it's sold.
5. Increases available expertise. By having the right team members on the sales call, questions raised by prospects can be immediately answered by experts.

▸ These advantages are only possible if you carefully manage the team selling situation. If it is not well-managed, you run these risks in team selling:

1. Confusion. This occurs when several of the sellers speak simultaneously or contradict each other. This is very bad for the sale.
2. Overwhelming the prospect. Do not bring your entire office on a sales call. Don't do anything that will create fear or overwhelm the buyer's side of the table.

▸ There are ten rules of effective team selling:

1. Select team members carefully.
2. Designate one person to orchestrate and lead the sale.
3. Meet beforehand to plan the agenda for the sale.
4. Have all team members prepare questions for the pre-briefing; that way, you're assured that all the vital questions can be sorted into the agenda.
5. Keep the number of people on your team to a minimum.
6. Answer questions succinctly.
7. Be flexible about your agenda.
8. Make sure all team members are on the same wavelength.
9. Be committed to selling something!
10. After the sale, meet again to discuss what worked and what didn't.

12

The "I Hate Selling" Professional's Black Bag Of Presentational Tools

This chapter sets forth in clear English the formal presentation and proposal process. These formal processes—sometimes referred to as dog and pony shows—are usually encountered only by larger firms for substantial clients, like publicly held or large private municipalities or large not-for-profits.

Even at this level of presentation or proposal—and perhaps it's most important here—please remember that *people buy other people*. In this chapter, you'll also learn how to respond to requests for proposals (RFPs).

In Chapters 10 and 11 we discussed more informal situations. This chapter considers conditions where a formal blockage has been placed between you (the seller) and them (the buyers). Often, buyers in this case are committees.

There is some bad news and some good news. The bad news is that this can be a lengthy and exhaustive process; the good news is that very few professional service providers have a grip on what it really takes to sell successfully in this area. You can improve your odds significantly by learning what some of the very top business producers in the professions do to bring in more business—despite this process.

A Brief Review

You'll want to test the formal presentation and proposal process in order to:

1. Invest your time effectively and get the business.
2. Satisfy the buyers' intellectual needs.
3. Give the buyers the opportunity to ask you questions.
4. Avoid wasting time and effort and giving away free ideas.
5. Give a custom-designed presentation or proposal (if necessary) that the buyer wants to hear.
6. Avoid talking yourself out of a sale.

We'll add one for this particular type of process:

7. Totally separate you from your competitors.

Selling to Committees

There are many downside risks in selling to committees:

- It is much more difficult to get a decision from a committee because there is more than one person involved.
- All of the people on a committee have different motives and egos to protect.
- You need to be more on your toes and more flexible than in any other selling situation.
- The committee decision-making process will take a much longer period of time than it would with only one decision-maker.
- Often, committees' decisions are already wired to a preferred person or firm. They bring in other firms to make their decision look like an objective process to protect themselves or for reasons related to the company policy of competitive bidding.
- Sometimes, committees are merely on fishing expeditions, and they are not in a position to be sold. These committees aren't buyers, they're thieves—stealing your time and good ideas. Use your sales examination to determine if they're serious about doing business (test for commitment to take action).

These downside risks create certain negative implications for you:

- You could waste billable hours selling to committees when you have no chance of success.
- You might be used by committees that aren't in a buying mode but rather are looking to be educated (for free). And/or they

might use you to obtain leverage to lower the price of their existing provider by getting other bids and proposals.
- You might become psychologically invested in the wrong situations, which can result in feelings of failure and rejection and serve as negative reinforcement to continue to sell your services.
- If you don't understand how to sell to individuals in a committee situation or the importance and implications of the committee's decision-making process, prospective clients will likely select your competition and you will lose more business than you should.
- Potential clients will continue to use firms that provide inappropriate service—because you didn't know their strategies for decisions or were not willing to take a risk.
- You may not secure other prospective clients who would buy, because you are wasting business development time with those who can't or won't buy.
- You look, act, and sound like your competition to the committee, thereby making the decision-making process incumbent upon fees.
- You lose the engagement by being more expensive than the prospective client expects.

If You Like Challenges, Committee Selling Is for You!

The most rigorous of all selling involves committees. The primary reason committees are tough to sell is that you will encounter several individuals, all of whom have different buying motives and egos to protect. To sell to any group, you must understand each member's motivation and present a package that relates to each of these interests as equally as possible. Few people enjoy it.

With committees, you may have to face from three to thirty people (not often thirty, thank goodness), all with different backgrounds within the organization they represent. They all bring different interests to the decision-making process. And, most important, they each have their own personal priorities. Certainly, they will tell you their main interest is the good of the company. But the committee member who works in the accounting function has one idea about what's good for the company, while the marketing department representative has another.

A second reason selling to a group gives one headaches is that committees practically force you to follow the prospective client's buying system rather than your selling system. In other words, they will try to force you to play by their rules. They'll attempt to place demands on you that suit their needs, without responding to any of your needs as a professional trying to do a thorough job.

For instance, you may get a directive from a committee describing the specifics they want included in a report. But, when you request more information, you hit a wall. Tension often builds as you struggle over whose system will prevail in this situation, but don't let anyone intimidate you or manipulate you.

Because you have to deal with so many individuals, it's more difficult to establish a mature, adult-to-adult relationship with these people. If you hope to sell to a group successfully, that should be your central goal when meeting with them.

A Prospective Client by Any Other Name . . .

The most effective strategy for selling to a committee is to forget you're selling to one. Think of the committee members as individual prospects. You cannot sell to a group en masse. You can, however, build a constituency by selling to each member as an individual.

The ideal situation is for you to interview members of the committee individually. Stress that individual meetings are a requirement for you to do a professional and efficient job. To get vital information, you need to speak with each member.

Explain that people are often inhibited in group situations. If you try to only interview the group as a whole, you will miss essential information and personal hurts and aches because someone was hesitant to bring up an issue in front of the other members. Or members may be distracted and not as attentive to your questions in a group situation. Therefore, you will not receive answers as complete as you would like.

You need to use your questioning skills to find out which aches exist with each member of that committee. That way, when you get them in the committee situation, you'll be comfortable and familiar with them personally, as well as with the dynamics of the group. You'll be in a much better situation to influence them as a committee. In order to reach that level of communication with them, you'll have had to speak individually with each member. Once you've won the support of individuals, you can sell them as a group.

In addition to giving you the information and emotional reasons you need to make a sale within the boundaries of your selling system, this strategy is an excellent way to differentiate yourself even more from the competition.

I promise you, most professional service providers do not interview individual members of committees making buying decisions. Most people assume it's not the way to do things; they certainly do not want to be perceived as pushy. They follow the common approach of selling to the group as a whole. They act as if the committee is one body, one prospect with one priority, one motivation, one ego. They will try to sell to the group en masse.

Remember, a key to success is not to look, act, or sound like the typical service provider. Going to each member of the committee with questions and requests will help you stand apart from the crowd. It will show that you are efficient, thorough, caring, prepared, and interested in their business. Aren't those great characteristics for a service provider to have?

And don't fool yourself: No matter who you are, there will be competitors who are (or at least appear to be) equally as good as you. So, if services are similar, and it's difficult for the prospective client to distinguish between them, you must be different. Take this opportunity to be different.

Most committee members will recognize that it takes guts for you to speak or meet with each of them. They will sense your commitment to doing a thorough job in your presentation, which will reflect a commitment to excellence in all areas of your work. The only drawback to this plan is that it's sometimes difficult to execute. And you may not want to invest the time up-front in order to accomplish the process effectively.

Sometimes, people on committees don't want to be sold individually. "What's a committee for, if individuals are being addressed?" they may say to you. If there are outside consultants involved in this selection process (who are competitors in disguise), they will usually try to prevent you from meeting with individual members of the committee. They want to keep you as subservient as possible, so that you feel unworthy to address individual members.

It is at this point that you must demonstrate your willingness to walk away from the situation in the event it seems to be turning manipulative on you.

Remember these facts if you hit serious resistance:

- *As you encounter resistance, understand that all the money being expended in this situation is not the prospective client's.* As a matter of fact, they only have to spend money when they find something they like. Remember that your cost of pursuing the sale is significant enough to warrant the individual involvement of committee members. You must not merely cast your fate to the wind. Your resources and time are too precious to expend where the outcome is entirely left to fate.

- *As a service provider, you make a living by offering a professional service.* You must understand the emotional objectives of each committee member in order to make the best diagnosis and do the most professional job. It's important that you not be expected to follow the prospects' system to the detriment of your objective, which is to serve the prospective client in the best manner possible and obtain the work for the firm. For you to do anything less would be the equivalent of sales malpractice.

When an Irresistible Force Hits an Immovable Object

There will be times when you do hit an immovable force that prevents you from reaching individual committee members. What should you do then? Consider these alternatives:

1. *You have the right to pass up the opportunity.* If you have a hard time reaching individual members, the chance to sell this group may not be so much an opportunity as a headache. Do you *need* the business? You're not going to starve to death tomorrow morning without it, are you? So, it may be logical to choose to move on to more reasonable prospects.

I've been a proponent of walking away from dangerous situations for a long time. Clients come to me often with problems similar to the unreachable committee described here. I almost always advise them to withdraw their bids, save their creative energies, and forget about the sale. Ninety-nine times out of a hundred, the ones who didn't listen find out the hard way.

Not understanding the emotional objectives of the individuals on a committee puts you at a terrible disadvantage. The committee maintains control of the selling situation, and you open yourself up to some serious manipulation. If you are able to close the business by some stroke of luck or simply because none of your competitors understood their objectives either, you risk establishing a relationship based on miscommunications, misunderstandings, and manipulation. Beware!

2. *You can sell to the person selling the committee.* Okay, if you're going to forge ahead, at least be equipped with some guidelines in

this risky territory. Let's say you decide that the prospective client is worth the trouble. The most desirable alternative is to sell to the person selling the committee as if he or she alone has the buying decision.

Usually when a committee is unreachable, they will have a single representative to mediate between them and the prospective service providers. Develop a relationship with that representative. Meet with that person, ask him questions, and discover his understanding of the committee's buying motives. Sell to those aches the same as you would to an individual.

Give your presentation to the mediating individual as though that person has the decision-making power. In essence, that's quite true. That person's opinion of the potential candidates will necessarily influence the decision the committee makes. His preferences will be reflected in the way he presents the proposals to the committee.

Once you finish your presentation, in lieu of closing the sale, get a commitment from that person to *sell*—not just *show*—your proposal to the committee. It's the next best thing to being there. The mediator is your link to selling the committee. Don't just give this person information to pass along to the group members; sell to him.

3. *You can request to be present when the committee makes its decision.* If you can be there when the committee is making their decision, you'll be the only service provider present. And to whom do you think they'll give their business if out of five competitors only one shows up to answer questions as they are making their decision?

They might come across problems and concerns as they review the proposals and consider final points. You can be the acting consultant. You can help them sort through the proposals. This strategy demonstrates your commitment to service and your desire to have the company as a client. Because you'll be the only professional to make this offer, once again you've differentiated yourself in a positive way from your competition.

All of my studies of buyers of professional services indicate that aggressiveness on the part of the service provider is a highly desirable trait. They want aggressive professionals who will be proactive with ideas for their business.

Even if you don't get the client this time around, you've positioned yourself as a professional with a commitment to excellence. The impression you've created will leave a door wide open for business in the future. Always keep that in mind. One sale is not the end of a relationship with a prospective client, regardless of whether you get the business the first time around.

4. *You can be last in making your presentation.* Being last has several advantages. First, as you begin your presentation, you can find out what they've liked and disliked about the competitors that have gone before you. This is vital if you've not had the opportunity to meet with individual committee members. You can profit from the mistakes of those service-providers who have preceded you. Don't feel bad about that. They would do the same thing to you, given the opportunity. That's the game of selling.

As you begin your presentation, you might ask if they have any needs that the other presentations have failed to address. This question works anytime you're not the first to make a presentation. Then you adapt your presentation to fill in those gaps and possibly offer some items no one else has.

This strategy works, even if you've been able to meet with members individually. It never hurts to be the last to give a presentation, as you are freshest and foremost in their mind; it increases your chances of getting the sale.

5. *You can offer to be first, last, and last again.* This is a powerful strategy for selling to committees. Simply ask to be the first to give your presentation. As you wrap up your presentation, ask the committee if they have any questions or any adjustments they would like to see in your proposal. Get a commitment from the committee to meet with you after they've seen and heard all the other presentations.

When you meet with them the last time, present your proposal again with the considerations mentioned during your first presentation. Then, in your final meeting—hopefully as they are making their decision—offer to assist in the evaluation of the proposals offered.

Once again, you're going beyond what the average service provider offers, you're setting yourself apart, and you're putting yourself in a position to have a strong influence on the committee's decision. What an excellent position from which to be selling! I suggest this strategy regardless of whether you've met with individual members.

Preparing for Formal Presentations

Here is a checklist culled from the top business producers in all of the professions to help you better prepare for formal presentations and increase your closing percentage:

- Interview everyone possible. In addition to the actual decision-makers, anyone who will be involved with the future service-provider (the user decision-makers and influencers) is a good source to find out what the real aches in the organization are. Once you find out what's really going on, you'll be in a better position to determine if there is a serious buyer and whether you are best capable of handling their situation.
- Get a coach and discover exactly what your presentation should be to get the business.
- Select a dynamic team that really wants the business. If any members of your presentation team are not as outrageously excited about securing the new client as you are, replace them with someone who is. This is one of the most common mistakes professionals make in the formal presentation situation: People are selected for the team based on their location, expertise, or availability, without a thought as to how they feel about getting the job. Overworked people who don't want any more time demands convey that message to the prospective client consciously and subconsciously.
- Have an ache brainstorming session. Sit down with your team after interviews have been done. Put together all of the client's aches. Then, with the help of your coach, you can best decide on what items to cover in your presentation.
- Select a quarterback. Someone is going to have to control presentation preparation process and the presentation when it is conducted. Free-for-alls do not impress future clients.
- Assign questions to ask and roles to play. Everyone on the presentation team should know what their role is going in. Assign them questions to ask the buyers to show their importance on the team as well as their interest in the client.
- Package a product based on fees. One of the keys to selling an intangible product is to package it and make it more substantial. Tell the buyers *exactly* what they will get if you are hired without going into boring details. Detail the features of the product and explain how it will help them to reach their goals better.
- Prepare a profile of the decision-makers. Everyone on your presentation team should know who they are talking to and what their roles and aches are.
- Bring them something new. What are the hot issues in their industry? Find out in your interviews and in industry-related publications and associations. Then supply them with an idea

they haven't thought of to help them better run their organization (without giving away how to accomplish it).
- Prepare a presentation workbook. Find out what they will want to see in the presentation workbook They should have some written visual materials to refer to that don't distract from your presentation.
- Practice at least once in front of an objective third party. You'll be amazed how much of the discomfort goes away after you've done a dress rehearsal with third parties acting as the buyers.

Here are some rules for conducting formal presentations:

- Get there early and socialize. The more human contact you have, the more likely it is you'll win the sale.
- Stay afterward and socialize. People buy other people. Find out what they liked. How did they react to the presentation team members? Where might there be a change? Do they want more input?
- Meet with your team before the appointment. Stage a pre-briefing to make sure everyone is on line. Give them a pep talk. Discuss their fears and concerns going into the room and they'll feel more at ease, thus giving a better impression.
- Don't sell; act like consulting physicians and make it a working session, not entertainment. That's right! Put the buyers to work! Find out in a group setting what their major concerns are; discuss their conditions of satisfaction. Create interaction and get them emotionally involved. Your competition will go in there selling and telling them about their two thousand offices all over the world . . . blah, blah, blah. Show them how you work with your clients to better their businesses. Ask them questions. Get a discussion going. Speak and respond into their aches. Spice it up; make it exciting and lively.
- Show off the workers. Display your teammates' expertise. Everyone should share in the presentation. Have them discuss case histories in similar situations without going into boring details or giving away your precious secrets or methodologies.
- Get a decision. Find out where you are in the process. If you have done your homework, are in front of real buyers, and did a great job on involving them in a working session, why should they hire anyone else? Find out how it went, right then and there. Be prepared to stay longer than you'd planned.

After the presentation:

- Debrief team members immediately. Find out at once what worked and what didn't. Get everyone's impressions down on paper. What should be done to follow through? Who will do what? What should you do more of next time? Congratulate them on an outstanding effort. Stay away from the negatives, or they won't want to do it next time.
- Set a follow-up meeting with your team to brainstorm with more new ideas for the client. The more personal contact you have with the prospective client, the more likely you are to win. New ideas are a great way to get back with the client and create additional powerful impressions.
- Change your team for next time. While it's still fresh, make a commitment to yourself to field a better team next time if it's warranted.
- Assign and send personal notes and follow up personal contacts. People love personal notes; it's just another way to totally separate you from everyone else.
- Follow through with promised information. Deliver it in person.
- Follow through immediately with your coach for input. Where are you as compared to the others? What's it going to take to complete the sale? Have any of your rivals got a leg up?
- Follow through for a decision. You should have been told when they were going to make a final decision (if not right then and there). Don't wait to be called; it's your job to get the decision. What if they don't respond to your call? That usually isn't a good sign, but something may have come up. Back off for a couple of days and call again.

I Hate Proposals and Requests for Proposals

I avoid doing proposals. My experiences, and those of many other professional service providers, have shown me that offering to do a proposal for a prospective client (or an existing client regarding additional work) can be a sure-fire way to cool off a hot prospective client and probably confuse them with detail and bore them to tears.

Do you believe that prospective clients actually read and study proposals? Some (very, very few—usually accountants or engineers) do. Most don't. In selling intangible professional services, people buy other people, not pieces of paper. Many times people buy despite proposals, rather than because of them. Therefore, we must spend a lot of time with prospective clients, getting to know them and what they need and want, rather than on writing proposals.

Don't get too excited over requests for proposals (RFPs), either. Experience teaches us that when a company sends an invitation to participate in a bidding process, you need to tread very carefully. There are many downside risks of proposal writing:

- Professional service providers often see proposals as a selling tool and expect the proposal to impress and persuade the prospective client and secure the business.
- Professionals assume that the prospective client needs to see a proposal in order to make a decision.
- Proposals are often used as free research or as a bargaining tool with the existing service firm.
- Many situations are wired to favor a particular firm, and securing proposals from other firms is a way of justifying the hiring of the wired firm.
- Written proposals often play a very minor part in the decision to purchase services.
- Proposals are often written in a language that the client doesn't understand.
- When a prospective client requests a proposal, it can often be a nice way to reject the service provider.
- Blind RFPs are usually a tremendous waste of time and money.

These downside risks create certain negative implications for you:

- You can lose many opportunities for generating new business because the prospective client cooled off while you were away writing an unnecessary proposal.
- You can waste enormous amounts of billable time writing a proposal that won't turn into business.
- You can become psychologically invested in the wrong situation, which can result in feelings of failure and rejection and serve as negative reinforcement to continue selling your services.
- You may give away your expertise to your competition and to people that have no intention of hiring you in the first place.
- You may fail to provide service and contact with existing clients because you are busy writing unnecessary proposals.

- You may not secure prospective clients who would buy because you are wasting business development time writing proposals.
- You may blame the proposal and the proposal writers for not securing the business instead of learning from your mistakes.
- You can place too much emphasis on the proposal to sell the business and not enough on developing the human relationship element, which is what really sells the work.
- You may turn off potential clients by communicating to them in jargon they don't understand in the proposal.

Approaching the Proposal Process

To be more successful at writing proposals, stop thinking like a professional service provider! Instead, start thinking like your entrepreneurial clients. How do they make decisions? Do they pour over reports? Do they spend hours in the library studying a subject? Do they wait weeks before making up their mind to do something? Most probably don't (unless your clients are attorneys).

Through the experiences of the top business producers in the professions, my own personal experiences, and those of my clients, I can assure you that decisions to buy are made at the human and emotional level, not at the paper level.

Art, one of the best business producers for over twenty years at a huge consulting firm, put it best:

> I don't get involved in proposal writing unless the prospective client needs to see something to formalize the agreement. Then I turn the proposal into an engagement letter, merely summarizing what we will do for them.
>
> I never, ever want to get involved in the proposal writing game. I've found, over a twenty-year period of creating millions of dollars of fees for the firm, that people buy other people. Prospective clients make up their minds in the first meeting as to who they *feel* they want to go with. It's my job to sell myself and my team to them at the first meeting. Unless I feel that the meeting went well and they tell me exactly where I stand in relation to my competitors and I am the front-runner, I decline the proposal process. We're just too busy to get involved in that. I've never sold any work where I didn't have that feeling of acceptance

during and after the meeting, no matter how great our proposal was.

Also, I never, ever offer to do proposals. Early in my career I thought it was professional to leave the sales call by offering the prospective client something in writing. What I was really doing was giving in to my own fear of requesting a decision from the client to move ahead on the project. I was afraid of hearing the word *no*, so I postponed the pain of possible failure by delaying the decision process.

What happened was that I left thousands of dollars on the table that could have been sold but weren't, because of my own fears. Often, I'd be with a prospective client, and they would be very excited about moving forward, about hiring us. By the time they had received the proposal, they had become reinvolved in their own lives and forgotten about me! I found that I couldn't get through to talk to them! They wouldn't return my calls. I was very confused; I thought that this was the way business was supposed to be done.

I also noticed that if by chance the prospect hadn't turned cold on me and still wanted to work with us after they had reviewed our proposal, they had invariably cooled off sufficiently from our original conversation so that fees were now an issue. I've found that once people detach from their problems for a while, they become less willing to pay us for what it's going to take to fix their situation properly, and we wound up reducing our fees to still get the business. That was very discouraging. I felt like some kind of peddler when I had to play price games with prospective and existing clients.

Fortunately, I ran into one of my formerly hot prospects at a chamber of commerce luncheon. I asked him point-blank why he wouldn't return my calls. He said that he thought I was being unprofessional by not offering to do the work he wanted done right away! He said that anyone that didn't have the common sense to close someone who wanted to do business wasn't the kind of person he wanted to be involved with. He also said that fees weren't an issue at our original discussion, but he really wasn't interested at any price now.

That experience taught me a very valuable lesson: get

them while they're hot. If you sense that the clients are serious about solving their problems or achieving their desires, set dates to start right then and there. Never, ever offer to do a proposal.

How does Art's advice apply to you? Consider these suggestions:

1. Don't offer to do proposals as a matter of course. Never back off from getting a decision to move ahead because you are afraid.
2. Don't get involved in the proposal game unless you feel you have a really good shot at getting the work. Pick and choose those proposal opportunities that you want to be involved in, based on your diagnosis of the chances of success in the situation.
3. Realize that the prospective client is buying people, not paper. The decision to do business with one firm over another is often made at the very first meeting and has very little to do with the magnanimity or brilliance of a document.
4. Fee issues become much more important the farther away you get from the initial conversation as the prospective client cools off. Get fees out of the way at the first meeting while the clients are still hot.

Writing Winning Proposals

Now, you've determined that a proposal is in order. You've conducted a sales examination to the best of your ability. You know the company's hurts, aches, desires, wants, needs, and musts; their fee expectations; and the decision-making process and your ability to influence it. There's good chemistry between you and people making or influencing the decision. There's a really good shot at getting the business. You've secured an internal mentor.

Whose proposal do you think they'll buy? Yours? Or theirs? The easiest proposal to sell is the one the client has written herself and will, therefore, help push through. Find out exactly from your coach what needs to be in the proposal based on her experience in the past and with these particular decision-makers. Outline it together. Ask her to review it before you submit it formally.

Put together your proposal and fax it to her, inviting comments and ideas. Request edits and criticisms. Have her fax it back to you.

Whose proposal is it now? Whose will be pushed internally and bought? If there is good chemistry, she will do this. If there isn't, or if they are merely fishing for ideas or using you as gambit to lower their current fees, watch out. You may be totally wasting your time.

A Different Animal: Requests for Proposals

There are several reasons to have misgivings about RFPs:

• Experience shows that a professional firm receiving an unsolicited RFP has a less than 5 percent chance of winning the business. RFPs are about two steps above raw cold calling, as far as your chances of immediately securing clients go.

• Responding to an RFP is expensive! Typically, the cost of responding to an RFP is between 5 percent and 20 percent of the gross dollars of the proposal. In other words, if you put together a $100,000 proposal, it'll typically cost you and your firm $5,000 to $20,000 to write that proposal. You have to consider the technical time, the document preparation time, and the time of the professional staff that has to be involved with the proposal. In addition to the in-house expense, you may have to involve an attorney to review the commitments requested in an RFP.

Responding to an RFP takes the service provider out of the business development game. When you work on a proposal for one company, you most likely will forgo other opportunities for business. Your cost in terms of time and energy is very high.

• Obviously, you weren't a part of the RFP process or the decision to request proposals from competing firms. The groups who were involved in that decision are looking out for their own interests, not yours. You are being asked to put together a proposal without meeting with the prospect or probing to discover that company's needs. For that reason, it's often difficult for you to pin down the motivation of the prospect.

Approach RFPs very carefully.

What to Watch Out for When Presented with an RFP

Why do companies send out requests for proposals? There are many reasons:

1. *There is a legitimate business opportunity.* Let's say a company's management recognizes that they have a problem with their current service provider. They believe they have defined it accurately and are now looking for someone to offer them a solution. So, they put together a set of specifics describing the problem and the guidelines for designing the solution. They then mail a request for a proposal to a list of firms that they believe could offer a solution. Their goal is to find the best possible resolution at the most reasonable price.

Some businesses are obligated to make major buying decisions through this process. Large project work and government business require RFPs and bids.

RFPs that fit this category are the least dangerous to respond to. If everyone is playing by the same rules, you at least have a fighting chance to win the business. But be careful: What looks like an even playing field may not be. Hash it over with others first (internal or external coaches) who may have experience with or input about the prospective client or a similar situation.

2. *Businesses are looking for information they believe you can provide.* It's a common ploy for decision-makers or consultants working with decision-makers to use RFPs to collect information. They might be working on a proposal of their own to present to a board of directors. By sending RFPs, they have a crack at your research and expertise for free. They also may get to see what their competition is up to.

And then there are the companies that send out RFPs that have no intention of changing service providers or doing anything, but are merely pricing the marketplace as a bargaining chip with their existing firm to lower their fees.

3. *Other consultants can justify their positions by involving several businesses in a competition for a contract.* Let's say a large hospital is looking for a computer system that can handle the hospital administration information systems plus all the patient information, and they have hired a consultant to help them shop around and make the final decision. That consultant is under pressure to bring the hospital bids from several firms. They will send out RFPs to generate a flurry of offers.

The danger here is that in many cases the consultants are aligned with one firm before the RFPs are ever mailed. For instance, a firm known as Computer Consultants may deal primarily with the data-processing division of the ABC firm. It is in the firm's best interest to sell ABC's system to the hospital. That firm has predetermined ABC will get the bid but needs to create the appearance of objectivity by considering several proposals. The RFP process also helps to justify the firm's existence as experts to sort through a maze of detail, as well as to create additional consulting fees.

If you happen to be the leading player in your field, one of the top firms in your industry, the firm probably needs your response for its own credibility. In that case, you may have some leverage.

Watch out for RFPs generated by a consultant. If you are being set up, you cannot win in this situation. Understand that a consultant environment is typically set up to make the outside resource feel that they are not a full participant in the selling process, that somehow they are less than equal to the consultant. When working through a consultant, you will often find it impossible to reach decision-makers.

How to Sell RFPs

Every RFP that lands on your desk shouldn't automatically be chucked into the nearest wastepaper basket. Consider two rules for responding to RFPs that can keep you out of trouble:

Rule 1. *Research the RFP and the company that generated it.* Interview and qualify anyone involved with the RFP and the final decision. Meet with the person who will be receiving the RFPs and making the final decision. Interview any consultants involved. Verify whether that business has ever selected your firm through the RFP process. Find out who they've chosen in the past for similar projects, and why.

Don't proceed until you're satisfied without a doubt that you have a level playing field and that you have a fair chance of earning the business. If you can't get all the information you need, or if someone refuses to meet with you or talk with you, you really need to consider whether you're willing to invest the resources it will take to respond with a proposal. If you don't think you can win, why bother?

Rule 2. *Submit an unsolicited response.* In other words, don't follow the specs and directions of the RFP. Instead, approach the business as you would any sale. Make sure you understand the real needs of the business, then propose a solution that will get the job done. Ignore the constraints of the RFP. This approach can work once it is established that you're working within a situation that can be won.

RFPs are a part of business. It's inevitable that they will be offered to you occasionally. Before you answer them, just make sure the opportunity exists for you to win, then discover for yourself—not necessarily relying on the information provided in the RFP—what it will take to win the business. Also, never mail a proposal. Proposals must be hand-delivered and reviewed with the parties that have requested it.

Case Study: How Not to Respond to RFPs

Bonnie headed up the computer consulting division of a large firm. One day, she received an RFP in the mail from a sister nonprofit organization of a large client in her city. Her office had successfully installed a new computer system at the local nonprofit organization two years earlier.

Without even picking up the phone, Bonnie and her crew went to work. Six weeks and two thousand hours of her staff's unpaid overtime and wasted weekends later, her team had produced a 327-page proposal that they shipped off to the other city. A real work of art!

Months passed without a word. When would they be starting work? Finally, at the behest of her boss, Bonnie wrote a letter to the nonprofit. Two weeks later she heard back; her firm hadn't even made the cut! Her proposal hadn't even been read; they had simply turned to the last page to see her estimated project cost, a casual $1.5 million. Everybody else was coming in around $250,000.

Net result: Bonnie's staff was totally demoralized, her boss extremely upset, and she left the firm soon thereafter.

Case Study: A Winning Response to an RFP

The XYZ Firm had conducted the legal work for the city of Springfield for fifteen years. Every three years the City Commission would put out RFPs for the legal work and every three years XYZ would keep it. By all signs the city was pleased that the XYZ firm did a technically competent job. The partner in charge of the client was considered an expert in the field of government law and municipal bodies.

The managing partner of the QRS Firm, Clyde, finally learned his lesson. Three years earlier after another loss, he made a commitment to get to know everyone on the City Commission who decided which firm was hired. This wasn't that difficult to do because he was already active in the city's major organizations. All that was required was to get next to the movers and shakers.

Clyde started joining committees that he knew would expose him personally to commission members. He took active, leadership roles that displayed his vitality and business common sense. He showed that he was far more than a municipal attorney by being proactive and aggressive toward solving problems and coming up with solutions.

Three years later he reaped the bonanza of his investment. Because he had become well acquainted with most of the members of the city commission, he was able to best direct his marketing person on the kind of written proposal to put together. His presentation team was well informed about the critical issues the city was facing and how they, as the city attorneys, could help. Although the city commissioners were not displeased with their current law firm, Clyde's firm was awarded the legal work because they wanted someone like Clyde "on their team."

What You Accomplished in Steps 6 and 7: The Formal Presentation and Proposal Process

You satisfied the reasons for testing the proposal and presentation process:

1. You did the work necessary to get the business (and not any more).
2. You satisfied the buyers' intellectual needs.
3. You gave the buyers the opportunity to ask you questions.
4. You avoided wasting time and effort and giving away free ideas.
5. You conducted a custom-designed presentation or proposal that the buyers wanted to see.
6. You didn't talk yourself out of a sale.
7. You separated yourself from the competition.

How to Proceed in the Sales Interview After the Formal Presentation

In Step 6, you tested to see if a presentation or a proposal was necessary, and you found out what a proposal would look like. In Step 7 you conducted a presentation or wrote a proposal that the buyers wanted to see. Now you need to proceed immediately to Step 8 and the formalization of the agreement: closure.

Diagnosis and Rx: Take Charge to Complete a Healthy Sale *and* Know When to Pull the Plug

Presentations:

- There are many downside risks in selling to committees:

  - It is much more difficult to get a decision from a committee because there is more than one person involved.

- All of the people on a committee have different motives and egos to protect.
- You need to be more on your toes and more flexible than in any other selling situation.
- The committee decision-making process will take a much longer period of time than it will with only one decision-maker.
- Often, committees' decisions are already wired to a preferred person or firm.
- Sometimes, committees are merely on fishing expeditions, and they are not in a position to be sold.

➤ These downside risks create certain negative implications for you:

- You could waste billable hours selling to committees when you have no chance of success.
- You might be used by committees that aren't really in a buying mode (they are just looking for a free education or price comparisons).
- You might become psychologically invested in the wrong situations.
- If you don't understand how to sell to individuals in a committee situation, you'll likely lose the sale.
- Potential clients will continue to use firms that provide inappropriate service, because you didn't know their strategies for decisions or were not willing to take a risk.
- You may not secure other prospective clients who would buy, because you are wasting business development time with those who can't or won't buy.
- You look, act, and sound like your competition to the committee, thereby making the decision-making process incumbent upon fees.
- You lose the engagement by being more expensive than the prospect expects.

➤ The most effective way to sell to a committee is to forget you're selling to one; think of all the committee members as individual prospects and sell each of them accordingly.

➤ If you hit serious resistance in your sales examination, remember:

- All the money being expended in this situation is not the prospective client's. At this point, you most likely have a significant investment in this sales process; the client's team only has to spend money when they find something they like. To warrant your investment, you must have some control.

- As a service provider, you make a living by offering a professional service. You must understand the emotional objectives of each committee member in order to make the best diagnosis and do the most professional job.

➤ If you find that you've hit an immovable force that prevents you from reaching individual committee members, these are your choices:

1. You have the right to pass up the opportunity.
2. You can sell to the person selling the committee. If you can't get past the mediator to each committee member, sell this liaison as you would in any other sale. Become the liaison's most trusted provider, and have that individual sell for you.
3. You can request to be present when the committee makes its decision.
4. You can be last in presenting your proposal and making your presentation.
5. You can offer to be first, last, and last again. Ask to be first, then after your presentation ask to come back again (last) to clear up any questions that arose. At that time, ask to be present when the committee makes its decision.

➤ To prepare for a formal presentation:

- Interview everyone possible, including decision-makers and anyone who will be involved with the future service-provider.
- Get a coach and discover exactly what your presentation should be to get the business.
- Select a dynamic presentation team that really wants the business.
- Have an ache brainstorming session.
- Select a quarterback, someone to control the process and the actual presentation.
- Assign questions to ask and roles to play.
- Package a product based on fees.
- Prepare a profile of the decision-makers.
- Bring them something new—research the hot issues in their industry and supply them with a fresh idea to help them better

run their organization (without giving away how to accomplish it).
- Prepare a presentation workbook.
- Practice at least once in front of an objective third party.

▸ Rules for conducting formal persentations:

1. Get there early and socialize—the more human contact you have, the more likely it is you'll win the sale.
2. Stay afterward and socialize.
3. Meet with your team before the appointment and pre-brief them to make sure everyone's on line.
4. Don't sell; act like consulting physicians—make it a working session, not entertainment.
5. Show off your teammates' expertise.
6. Get a decision.

▸ After the presentation:

- Debrief team members immediately; find out at once what worked and what didn't.
- Set a follow-up meeting with your team to brainstorm with more new ideas for the client.
- If the presentation didn't go well, make a commitment to change your team for next time.
- Assign and send personal notes and follow up with personal contacts.
- Follow through with promised information, and deliver it in person.
- Contact your coach immediately for feedback.
- Follow through for a decision.

Proposals:

▸ There are many downside risks of proposal writing:

- Professional service providers often see proposals as a selling tool and expect the proposal to sell the prospective client.
- Professionals assume that the prospective client needs to see a proposal in order to make a decision.
- Proposals are often used as free research or as a bargaining tool with the existing service firm.

- Many situations are wired to favor a particular firm, and securing proposals from other firms is a means to justify the hiring of the wired firm.
- Written proposals often play a very minor part in the decision to purchase services.
- Proposals are often written in a language that the client doesn't understand.
- When a prospective client requests a proposal, it can be a nice way to reject the service provider.
- Blind RFPs are usually a tremendous waste of time and money.

➤ These downside risks create certain negative implications for you. You can:

- Lose new business because the prospective client cooled off while you were away writing an unnecessary proposal
- Waste enormous amounts of billable time writing a proposal that won't turn into business
- Make a psychological investment in the wrong situation, resulting in negative reinforcement to continue selling your services
- Give away your expertise to your competition and to people that really have no intention of hiring you
- Neglect existing clients because you were busy writing unnecessary proposals
- Miss selling to prospective clients who would buy because you are wasting business development time writing proposals
- Blame the proposal and the proposal writers for not securing the business instead of learning from your mistakes
- Place too much emphasis on the proposal to sell the business
- Turn off potential clients by confusing them with jargon in the proposal

➤ Since proposals can have many negative implications, don't offer to do proposals as a matter of course, and don't get involved in the proposal process unless you feel you have a really good shot at getting the work. Be sure to remember that the prospect is buying a person, not a piece of paper, and that fee issues become much more important as time goes by and the client cools off.

➤ If you do write a proposal, make sure that it is one the prospect will want to see. Work closely with the decision-makers and let them tell you exactly how to structure your proposal.

▸ There are several reasons to have misgivings about RFPs: professional firms that receive unsolicited RFPs general have a very low chance of winning the business; responding to an RFP is expensive; and you were not involved in the RFP process, so it's often difficult to pinpoint the genuine motivations of the prospects.

▸ Companies send out RFP's because:

1. There is a legitimate business opportunity.
2. They are looking for information they believe you can provide.
3. Other consultants can justify their positions by involving several businesses in a competition for a contract.

▸ Before you discard an RFP, research the company who generated it. Do your best to take control of the process, and don't respond unless you're satisfied that you have a fair chance of earning the business. Or you can also submit an unsolicited response; that is, don't follow the directions of the RFP. Instead, approach the business as you would in any sale.

13

Rx for Sure-Fire Closes—Just What The Professional Orders

In this chapter you'll learn how to close the business and complete the sales audit. The purposes of Step 8: Finalize the Agreement are to:

1. Formalize and complete the agreement. Until you have a signed engagement letter, what have you really got? In this step you will *painlessly* close your patient and also tie up any loose ends that could keep you from proceeding.
2. Bypass bad emotional swings and to ensure that you get 'em while they're hot. If you've ever had prospective clients sit on engagement letters without signing them, you know what I mean.
3. Avoid bad feelings about selling. There are few things worse in selling than to lose one you thought you had. In this step you will secure a commitment to move forward and create closure.
4. Circumvent buyer's remorse and elude back-outs and mind-changers.
5. Secure a referral. Closing deals is often the best time to get a referral, as the new client feels relieved and positive about having made a decision to remove her aches.

What Is Closing?

Closing is the logical progression of an effective process. Throughout the sales examination process, you have been testing your patient and moving ahead or stopping. If the patient had certain characteristics, such as emotional reasons for doing something, commitment to be healed, willingness to pay, you progressed to the next step.

Like a physician, now you've arrived at the point where it only makes sense to schedule the operation and do the work. It would not be logical to make the patient wait to be healed, although there is a possibility that the patient may get cold feet and change her mind. Therefore, closure is the perfectly rational conclusion to the sales examination.

Actually, you've been closing throughout the sale—perhaps without realizing it. Closing, contrary to misconceptions, is not a great leap by the prospective client or by you. From the very moment you endeavored to establish chemistry and discover their hurts, you were closing the buyers. When they allowed you to lead the conversation, when they agreed to tell you where it hurt, they were closing themselves as to whether to move ahead with you as their business physician.

How to Complete the Sale: Methods You Can Use to Finalize the Agreement and Secure Closure

You want to finalize the agreement as painlessly as possible. Any resemblance to what a stereotypical salesperson would do may scare off your buyer. Avoid trial closes like, "Would Tuesday at 9:00 or Thursday at 2:00 be better for you, sir?" or, "If you decided to buy, which would you prefer, the three zillion megabyte or the four?" Ugh!

Your clients are closed that way every day of the week. Avoid the behavior of those ineffective salespeople so you don't ruin your image and scare off clients. The close should be invisible, natural, and logical; here are two ways to close painlessly:

1. *Use silence.* This is my favorite way to finalize. The sales examination process is so sensible for buyers, that, after you have completed the tests, many will say some form of, "Well, I guess we should move ahead. . . ." Beautiful. People don't object to their own ideas.

2. *Set dates.* My second favorite approach. If people don't close themselves within a minute or two after I stop presenting, I ask to set dates.

Look, you're a professional service provider. What you sell is time, yours or other people's. You're booked ahead with other commitments. It only makes sense to set dates now to avoid telephone tag and those unforeseen events that always seem to come up. At the appropriate time, say something like, "Ted, can we go ahead and set some dates? My schedule is filling up."

Set a date right now to get that engagement letter over to them, reviewed with them, and signed. Don't mail engagement letters— you've invested too much effort to take a chance to blow it now. If they are in another city, consider faxing it to them or send it overnight. Follow through and review it with them on the phone immediately.

What if you can't set solid dates? Set "tentative" dates instead, as in Bernie's conversation with Ms. Jones:

Bernie: Can we set a date for the first strategic planning session?
Jones: I've promised to meet with Joe before we make any final decision. I owe him that much.
Audrey: Can we set some tentative dates then? That way I can have my calendar clear in case you decide to move forward.
Jones: That makes sense.

If you can't even set tentative dates, you're in big trouble. And you can always look back to the previous examination steps to find out what went wrong. Was there enough chemistry? Did they hurt bad enough? Are they committed? Did you clear fees? Are these people in a position to make a decision? Was something not covered the way they would like it in the presentation? If you can't set the tentative dates, then you need to jockey for last again (see Chapter 9).

Here are some thoughts to remember regarding closure:

• *A decision not to make a decision . . . is a decision!* When those few people at the end of this process tell you that they need more time to make a decision, guess what: They just have made a decision (to do nothing). Which way will they swing if they are in the positive position right now? That's why giving the buyer the logical opportunity to set dates now is so important.

• *No is the second best word you can hear.* You have permission to fail when selling! You must fail at times to succeed more (nobody ever bats 1.000 in this game). In case you're wondering, the best word you can hear is yes. But, you knew that; you've almost finished the book!

• *Don't get in a game of tag, you're it.* Some people just don't have the heart to tell you no, so they lead you along for a couple of lifetimes hoping you give up or they move on to another job. Ever play this game? It sounds like this:

Buyer: Terry, why don't you give me a call in a couple of weeks.

You wait two weeks, call back six times, finally get through, and if she remembers you:

Buyer: You know, now isn't a good time. My husband is going to Yugoslavia for a couple of months. Give me a call around April 1st.

April 1st rolls around:

Buyer: Terry? Who? Oh yes, uh, we're still waiting for budgets to come out. Give me a call at the beginning of June.

June 1st:

Buyer: I'm so sorry. The kids are home from school and we're going away.

September 1st:

Buyer: Gosh, the kids are going back to school and the cat died. . . .

You get the picture. Nothing feels worse in selling than to be led on. What do do? Apply Step 8 now, while you are in their office, before they forget where it hurts and who you are.

• *Never offer to do a proposal.* I've said it before, but just for some reinforcement, under penalty of death, never offer to do a proposal when people are ready to be closed.

Most businesspeople aren't accountants or engineers. Businesspeople are generally not risk-averse; they make decisions daily. You are like a dentist who has qualified her patient by finding out where it hurts, discussing fees, and by knowing the decision-making process. Be prepared to pull the tooth *now*.

Can you imagine a dentist saying, "I'm sorry, I can't pull your tooth because I'd rather do a proposal first." Professional service providers do this every day, losing more sales they would have won because they didn't know the client was sold and were too shy to close the sale.

If you don't close the deal, these things might happen:

1. The hurt could go away. Sound familiar? Maybe you've even gone to the dentist or set an appointment but the pain went away. As illogical as it sounds, some people back out of those appointments and don't get their teeth fixed.
2. The patient feels teased and gets upset with you. Hurt causes closure by itself! People are self-motivated when they are uncomfortable; they want to take care of what ails them. That's one reason it is so important to find out if the buyers have hurts in the first place. If they don't, they won't act. If you don't step forward to alleviate their aches, they may get mad at you and go elsewhere!
3. Willingness to pay fees decreases dramatically. The longer you wait after the initial interview, the less your solution will be worth to the client.

Handling Stalls and Objections

I hate stalls and objections. Salespeople are taught to welcome stalls and objections as buyer's signals. Ha! Wonder what insane person thought that up?

The sales examination is purposely designed to get reasons for not doing the business out of the way early and avoid wasted time, unnecessary work, and your bad feelings. Don't expect to hear stalls and objections after you have completed the examination. Ninety percent of the time, you will be able to set dates and move forward.

In the sales examination you've addressed fees—up front. You've addressed the decision-making process—up front. You've addressed commitment, emotional needs, wants, desires, and musts--up front. People who aren't ready to go at this point are either dead, insane, or masters at jerking people around. Or something may still be missing that they may feel uncomfortable about (don't expect it, but know how to deal with it just in case).

A Systematic Approach to Overcoming Stalls and Objections

1. Get specific. Precisely identify the hold-back to moving forward.
2. Ask, "Why is that important?" Find out why this particular

reason is meaningful to the buyer. You can deal with it only
by precisely identifying it and determining its significance.
People who aren't willing to share this with you aren't serious
buyers—you should move on to someone who is.
3. Discover the other objections they might have. Identify and
list these now.
4. Ask, "What if?" Ask the buyer, "If I can deal with these issues, will I get the business?" If they say no, you're wasting
your time. If they say yes, secure their commitment, answer
their concerns, set dates, and close the deal now.

Avoiding Back-Outs and Mind-Changers

Ever have a prospective client change his mind after you've invested
your energy, time, heart, and soul into the process? Few things are
more disappointing than losing one you thought you'd won. Often,
it's our own fault that the sale is lost. It happens because we haven't
dealt with the inevitable buyer's remorse that occurs after someone
buys something.

You know what I'm talking about! You're driving out of the dealership with a brand new $28,000 car and you say to yourself: "Oh my
gosh! What have I done? Did I really need to spend all that money on
a car?"

Same thing happens to your buyers, too. If you've done a good
job of conducting the sales examination, it should happen less and
less, but—just in case—deal with it now, while you're still with the
buyer, after he's closed. Dealing with mind-changing now doesn't
absolutely guarantee that people still won't back out of their commitments; it just lowers the chances of it happening.

Bernie did an excellent job of dealing with back-out possibility in
his conversation with Ms. Jones and Bob:

Bernie: What do you think Joe will say when he finds out you've
hired us? When do you plan on telling him?
Jones: He'll have a fit. We're his biggest client. I need to tell him
right away.
Bernie: What do you think he'll do?
Bob: Oh, he'll beg, promise, and possibly even cry. We tried to
change CPAs about six years ago and he wound up keeping the
work.
Bernie: Ms. Jones, what do you think will happen?
Jones: Bob's right.

Bernie: Do you think you'll keep Joe again?

Bob: I don't see how we can. It's hurting me, my people, and our business.

Jones: Painful as it will be, we must go through with it.

Bernie: How can I help?

Jones: I'm not sure.

Bernie: We can make the transition as easy as possible, and there are times, of course, when we run into business that is simply too small for us to handle. After we get done reviewing Joe's records and meeting with him, if I like what I see, we might be able to start referring some small business to him as the need arises.

Jones: That would be nice.

Bernie: Here's my experience in similar situations. Right now you see a need to trade up to a bigger firm that will give you better all-around service. Joe's not going to let this go under any circumstances. Old relationships are very hard to break.

Before you say no, I suggest you turn Joe's next appointment into a transition meeting. I'll stop by with an engagement letter Monday morning on the way in to work. I hope I'm not being too forward, but this is an emotional issue that must be dealt with directly. If you have engaged us, there's not much Joe can do.

Jones: I don't know . . .

Bob: I do. We must make a change. We need Bernie and Audrey's firm, or we're holding back our business and hurting our employees, like Mary and me.

Jones: All right.

In this example Bernie pulled out all of the stops. What would have happened if he hadn't? A good question to ask after closing the deal is, "Is there anything that might prevent us from moving forward?"

Getting Referrals at Closure

After closing the deal is a great time to ask for referrals. People feel good when they've made a decision to remove their aches. Decision-making by itself is a self-esteem booster. At this delicate point, they feel confident in themselves and in your ability to help them.

Often, people will naturally tell others when they've taken action: "Jim, I just bought a new car." "Jane, I found a wonderful new doctor." It makes them look smart to themselves and they're looking to validate (even brag) about their decision to others.

No, you haven't done any work for them yet. Remember, your clients probably think differently than you do. They most likely won't be able to recognize technical expertise in making their decision— they buy other people and they've bought *you.*

The top business producers have built their practices on referrals from new clients, existing clients, and contacts. They know that to wait for referrals is a sure way to stagnate their business. They ask early and often.

Isn't it demeaning to ask for referrals? Says who? This is the 1990s, not the 1950s. Business goes to those who pursue it. Besides, how have your clients built their businesses? Through word of mouth advertising and referrals! Businesspeople understand the power of referrals, and they will help you if they like and respect you.

Try this:

Service Provider: Ms. Rockefeller, do you know of anyone I should be talking to who may be in a situation similar to yours that we might be able to assist?

Three things will happen: She'll say either yes, no, or, "I'm not sure." If she says yes, find out who and ask her to make the introduction for you. If she says, "I'm not sure. . . ," ask her if you can follow through with her after she's had a chance to think about it.

Diagnosis and Rx: Be Sure to Complete
The Entire Examination

➤ Step 8 is Finalize the Agreement. Be sure to finish this step in order to:

1. Formalize and complete the agreement.
2. Bypass potential mood swings—get 'em while they're hot.
3. Avoid bad feelings about selling.
4. Circumvent buyer's remorse and eliminate back-outs.
5. Secure referrals.

➤ Closing is the logical progression of an effective process. Throughout the sales examination, you've been leading the prospect to this point; the close is simply the next logical step.

▸ The close should be invisible and natural; here are some ways to close painlessly:

1. Use silence—let the buyer suggest the next step.
2. Set dates: set solid or at least tentative dates to start the work.

▸ Some thoughts to remember regarding closure:

- A decision not to make a decision . . . is a decision.
- No is the second-best word you can hear.
- Don't get in a game of tag where you end up continually chasing the prospect for a decision.
- Never offer to do a proposal.

▸ If you don't close the sale at the appropriate time, three things can happen:

1. The hurt could go away.
2. The patient may feel teased and get upset with you.
3. The prospect's willingness to pay fees will decrease dramatically.

▸ Stalls and objections are reasons the prospect gives you for not doing business. The sales examination is designed to eliminate these intrusions.
▸ If you do hear stalls or objections, use this approach to overcoming them:

1. Get specific. Precisely identify the hold-back to moving forward.
2. Ask, "Why is that important?"
3. Discover what other objections the buyer might have.
4. Ask, "If I can deal with these issues, will I get the business?"

▸ After closing the deal is a great time to ask for referrals. People feel good about making a decision and will likely be pleased to give you a referral at this time.
▸ To request a referral, say something like:

Service Provider: Ms. Rockefeller, do you know of anyone I should be talking to who may be in a situation similar to yours that we might be able to assist?

▸ By following these steps to complete Step 8, you've accomplished the following:

1. You've formalized the agreement and closed the sale.
2. You've avoided bad emotional swings and got 'em while they were hot.
3. You've avoided bad feelings about selling.
4. You've circumvented buyer's remorse and eluded back-outs and mind-changers.
5. You've requested and perhaps secured a referral.

Congratulations! You have now completed the sales examination!

Part Three
Enhancing Your Selling

14

Triumphant Telephone Selling: Reach Out And Touch New Business Arteries

That little tool sitting atop your desk can be a very powerful business-development resource. In this chapter, you'll learn how to be more effective on the phone, the virtues and drawbacks of telephone selling, and what can be expected from it versus face-to-face communication.

Unless your clients are located in faraway places, the role of telephone selling is merely to set an appointment that the buyer will keep. Yes, you can enroll clients and sell additional work on the phone, but I don't recommend it over face-to-face interaction. You are selling an intangible service; you are only selling yourself. This is not a product people are accustomed to ordering over the phone!

However, the telephone offers some powerful benefits, when utilized properly, for your sales efforts:

- *Talking on the phone is like confession.* People will open up to you on the phone just like in a confessional. It's amazing. There is a physical barrier between you and the other party, so they feel safer talking to you.

- *You have their total attention.* Unless they have call waiting, you don't have to worry about being interrupted by phone calls! There are fewer distractions and you will have someone's full attention, if the call is handled correctly (more about that later).

• *It's faster.* Telephone selling takes approximately one-third the time face-to-face selling does. On the phone, people tend to get to the point more quickly.

• *Less can go wrong.* In communicating with others, the words you say are less important than the tones in which you speak and how you look and act. What if you are still wearing polyester suits from the 1970s? Need a haircut? Spilled coffee on your tie? Wear blue jeans to work? Who cares? They can't see you! It's easier to make a good impression on the phone, because less can go wrong!

• *You can separate yourself from the competition more easily and quickly and set the personal tone for future dealings.* A phone call to set an appointment, properly managed, will ensure that you'll be welcomed as an invited guest and warm acquaintance when you show up for the sales interview. Also, chances are that your competition hasn't a clue as to how to enroll clients on the phone. Some may have been trained to sell by salespeople on the phone, training that would likely act to their disfavor.

Unfortunately, the phone offers some negatives as well:

• You have about eight seconds to capture someone's attention.
• Voice mail and secretaries (also known as gatekeepers) can inhibit contact, unless you know how to get around them and utilize them to your benefit.

When to Use the Phone

There are many good times to use the phone. The following are particularly appropriate. Use the telephone to:

1. *Set appointments with hot leads.* The phone is most commonly used to set an appointment with red-hot leads like referrals. Some service providers are so scared of the phone or have their priorities so messed up that they don't even follow through on referrals received from clients and other sources!

But you are focused on building your business. Use the phone to set a date that won't be broken by either party, where you can discuss the prospective client's aches, fees, and so on.

If your party isn't in, take the responsibility of calling back. This removes any mind games about whether they will return your call.

2. *Maintain and improve contact with clients.* Another good way to use the phone is simply to maintain more contact with your clients. Although you personally may not like your work being interrupted by phone calls, you can improve almost all of your client relationships (thus earning additional business from them, higher fees, and more referrals) just by "reaching out and touching someone."

Using the phone effectively to help build my practice was a very difficult lesson for me to learn, because I hate being bothered when I am working on a project. But I've been taught by the best, applied it, and my clients say they like receiving regular calls. They always have time for me on the phone and like my checking in regularly just to see how they're doing.

The top business producers in the professions systematically call at least one client and/or a referral source every single day, no matter how busy they are. Many say it relieves the stress of daily business by giving them a required break from the grind of the day and keeps them more motivated.

3. *Reignite relationships and improve connections with referral sources.* Get out your personal address file and make ten calls a month to old friends, classmates, and others you haven't talked to in a while. Meet for breakfast or lunch. Remember, if you are out of sight, out of mind, it is most difficult for them to refer or do business with you. They are excellent referral sources only if they see or hear from you on a consistent basis. Remember Mary, your old college roommate? She may be a player at a major company by now. Call her up. How about Tony? He was just a struggling junior with you all too many years ago at Frick and Frack—maybe he doesn't want to do audits anymore in his sole proprietorship. Ring him up.

Be committed to make 120 calls a year to people who may be in a position to help you, and your business will grow dramatically. Chances are it's 120 calls more than your competitors are making.

4. *Set appointments with warm leads.* Use the phone to set appointments with people you meet who are not yet clients or referral sources but should be; lunches are the best vehicle for this. These people are warm because you know them and something about them. No, you won't bat 1.000 here either.

However, let's say you've interacted with Helen at the Society of the Brain-Dead for the last three years. You know she's got her own business but aren't sure about where she stands in relation to her service provider or what aches she may possibly have. It's time to pick up the phone, ask her to lunch, find out what other organizations she's involved with, and diagnostically test her to see if there's a match.

Consultant: Helen? Hi! It's Jack Johnson from the Society of the Brain-Dead. How are you?
Helen: Jack? Hi, how are you?
Consultant: Okay. The purpose of my call is to see if you're available for lunch next week. I've made it a habit of getting to know as many people as I can in the society; networking with others is so important these days. What's your calendar look like?

That's your close: "What's your calendar look like?" It's very subtle, yet direct, and it's proved phenomenally effective—I close almost 100 percent of these kinds of appointments. I don't use or recommend, "When are you available?"—it seems so many salespeople use that. Also, avoid at all costs alternative closes like: "Would you rather get together at 10 A.M. on Tuesday or 3 P.M. on Thursday?" I'm gagging even as those words are coming from my fingers! Don't ever apply ancient and common closes that dreaded salespeople use—if you do, you're setting yourself up for failure.

And consider this: Why shouldn't Helen meet with you for lunch? She'd be nuts not to. Everyone in business knows that professional service providers are great referral sources for them, too. You can have a mutually profitable conversation by gently probing and listening for her aches with her present service provider (reread Chapter 7) and by finding out more about her, so you can plug her in to your contacts if the need arises.

No, you might not secure her as a new client over lunch next week, but you can begin the process of qualification to see if she is someone you'd like to add to your client family in the near future. Remember, people buy other people—they often change service-providers for relationship and nontechnical reasons. Give her and others the opportunity to know who you are as a person away from the distractions of organizational meetings. Selling is an examination. You can't sort her in or out unless you test her first.

5. *Sell.* Yes, you can sell your service on the phone. I've had to over the years, because my clients are spread all over the world. People *will* hire you without meeting you in person. All of the selling methodologies discussed in this book can be modified for phone use.

Careful! Don't consider using the phone to sell unless you consider yourself an experienced and effective in-person closer. Also, don't be lazy; always visit prospective clients in person if they are geographically available. In-person meetings are always preferable to closing on the telephone.

Doing Your Own Telemarketing

Perhaps you're starting a practice from scratch, have moved to a new town, or just want to build your business. Only after you have exhausted every possible lead, referral, friend, relative, poker buddy, and fraternity brother or sister, should you consider making phone calls to total strangers.

Some professionals are attracted to telephone solicitation (conducted by others, of course) as an easy and painless way to build their practice. Hiring and managing telemarketers is very expensive, and it generally results in putting the professional in front of nonqualified prospects, thus wasting her time and energy.

However, if you have fully pursued all of the other ideas about how to market your practice most effectively, and you have a couple of hours a day on your hands at certain times of the year, you might want to try telemarketing yourself.

As always, there are advantages and disadvantages to doing your own telemarketing. On the plus side, you are in total control of the process. People will get to meet you, rather than some third party, on the phone. By doing your own phone work, you have the opportunity to engage a prospective client in a solid conversation about her business. You may discover some aches, hurts, needs, wants, desires, and musts she might not have realized she had or which simply weren't bothering her, until she had an opportunity to talk them through with you. Doing your own telemarketing gives the buyer the opportunity to get to like you. People meet with and hire people they know, like, and trust.

If you do your own telemarketing, you'll save time training and listening in on phone calls. And you might just do a better job on the phone than someone who doesn't have a personal interest in your practice.

On the other hand, the down sides are obvious. You're going to have to personally face the pain of rejection, failure, and hang-ups. You might feel it is unprofessional for someone who has worked as hard as you have to be a professional to resort to cold telephone calling. What will people think?

If you do want to make your own calls, I suggest using the following script with appropriate modifications for your own personal information. The direct approach works best. Get people talking—just as you would on any sales interview learned in this book—using informational questions first, then circling in on where it hurts. Here's a sample script I put together for one of my clients who wanted to do his own cold calling:

Secretary: XYZ Company.
You: Hi. John Smith, please. [*or*] Hi! Is John around?
Secretary: May I tell him who's calling?
You: Sure, it's Gus James.
Secretary: May I ask what this is in regard to?
You: I'd rather discuss this directly with John, if you don't mind. Thank you.
Smith: Hello, John Smith.
You: John? Hi! It's Gus James. How are you?
Smith: Fine. Who is this?
You: Gus James. The purpose of my call, John, is to find out if we should be meeting in person to discuss your business. I'm a local [*fill in the blank*], and one of the ways I get to meet people I don't know is to call them up and find out about them and their businesses. Do you already have a [*fill in the blank*]? Are you delighted with the level of service they give you? Or is it possible they could be providing more information faster and better?

> Often, I meet with future clients who aren't receiving the level of service they want from their [*fill in the blank*] or feel they just aren't getting their money's worth. Have you considered changing or would you consider receiving a second opinion on what services your current [*fill in the blank*] aren't providing for you?
Smith: Why, yes I have.
You: Good! Let's set an appointment. When are you available? Let's set a time to meet and discuss your situation.
Smith: Wednesday morning is fine.

Nine Ways to Overcome Phone Phobia: The Keys to Effective Telephone Selling

1. *Keep your phone calls conversational and casual.* Let people meet the real you on the phone. Remember that they may receive many calls from salespeople soliciting business, and you never want to sound like a salesperson, since you might scare your prospects away

and they may treat you like one. Rather, you want to be treated like the successful professional you are. Conduct your phone conversations as the top business producers do when they follow through on a lead—their phone calls sound much the same as conversations they have with their clients.

Also, secretaries and receptionists are trained to keep salespeople (and anyone who sounds like one) away from their bosses. You don't need additional barriers—get by these gatekeepers as quickly as possible. For example:

Consultant: Hi! Is Bill around?
Secretary: Sure, hold on please.

Eighty percent of the time, the secretary will put you right through because it sounds like you know him. And she's been told before not to screen out his golf buddies and friends. This casual approach works a heck of a lot better than the sales approach that secretaries respond to daily:

Consultant: Good morning. May I speak to Mr. William Wilson, please?
Secretary: What's this in regard to?
Consultant: I'm with ABC Computer Consultants. I'd like to speak with Mr. Wilson, please.
Secretary: He's busy and we've already got computer consultants.

You don't need to get into that foray. Use an informal approach:

Consultant: Hi! Is Bill around?

If the secretary is suspicious, she'll say:

Secretary: May I tell him who's calling?
Consultant: Sure, it's Art Smart.

The less information you give to secretaries and receptionists, the less ammunition you give them to shoot you down, make your life difficult, and waste your time. If the secretary persists:

Secretary: May I ask what this is in regard to?
Consultant: Of course. [*It doesn't hurt to sound just a little impatient here.*] Jill Twill told me to give Bill a call.

Better yet, if Jill was kind enough to telephone Bill to let him know you were calling:

Consultant: Of course. Bob's expecting my call.

An informal and casual tone always takes the edge off of telephone conversations and establishes chemistry more quickly.

2. *Use a little ingenuity to reach the prospect.* If you're afraid of dealing with secretaries, call when they aren't around: before eight-thirty or nine, at lunchtime, or after five. Call prospects on holidays—many catch up on their work then. Often the people you're trying to reach don't work easy nine-to-five schedules.

Make sure to treat every receptionist and secretary with the utmost respect. These people can keep you from getting through, but if you turn them into allies, they will go out of their way to help you. I always remind myself to be really friendly and make a good impression with the receptionist and secretary, often asking for their first name:

Secretary: Mr. Florida's office.
Me: Good morning. This is Allan Boress. Is Frank around?
Secretary: No, I'm sorry, he's not.
Me: And what is your name please?
Secretary: Mary.
Me: Mary, when's a good time to catch him?
Secretary: Oh, he'll be in later this afternoon.

Now, at that point, you can leave a message—which I don't recommend—or simply call back again. I don't recommend leaving messages because you don't want to play telephone tag. Also, the person may not know who you are or may be too distracted to return your call.

Secretary: Would you like to leave a message?
Me: No, thanks. I'm at a client's and can't be reached. I'll give Frank a call back later. Thank you.

Always remember that if you are nice to people (including secretaries and receptionists), the vast majority will go out of their way to help you. This seems to be especially true of support people, who tend to be underpaid, overworked, and rarely appreciated.

And what about voice mail? I love voice mail. It allows me to leave a detailed message at my convenience and not deal with a secretary at all. Often, when a secretary answers and the party I'm trying to get to isn't there, I ask if there is a voice-mail box. If so, I will leave a message that states my purpose for calling and prepares the prospect for my next call (so I have their attention when we do connect).

Put voice mail to work for you. Leave people a message telling them who you are, why you are calling, and exactly when they can expect your next call. Then they'll be better prepared to talk to you, and it won't be such a surprise when you call.

3. *Maintain a powerful physiognomy while on the phone.* Many professional service providers find their telephone conversations more effective and influential when they conduct the conversation while standing or pacing in their office rather than slouching and staring down at their desk.

How you stand, if you're sitting, whether you are looking down or your chin is up—all can affect the results of your conversations. This has to do with your physiognomy of posture—standing erect and looking up is more empowering and energizing than staring down into a phone or desk. An investment in a long telephone cord or a mobile phone could be a good investment.

4. *Ask yourself, "What would I do if I weren't afraid?"* Even the biggest rainmakers get that familiar twinge of fear occasionally when staring at the telephone. Next time that happens, let your actions and telephone conversations flow easily by first asking yourself, "What would I do if I weren't afraid?" Chances are you will reply to yourself, "Why, I'd pick up that phone right now and call. . . ."

It's amazing how asking this simple question of yourself dissipates the natural fear of using the telephone (especially when calling people you don't know that well), and it strengthens you to call now.

5. *Avoid Monday mornings for phone calls.* Monday mornings are a difficult time to catch someone's attention, especially when trying to create some chemistry or setting appointments. People are too distracted trying to settle in for their own work weeks.

I've found that Friday afternoons are a good time to set appointments. At that time, most people are winding down from a hectic week, and they tend to be more relaxed and receptive. However, don't make the mistake of holding all of your calls to Fridays—you're going to find that a lot of people aren't around.

6. *Don't worry about interrupting people.* Nine out of ten times, your phone call won't interrupt someone who can't talk to you or give

you undivided attention. You may want to ask the other party if they have a few minutes to talk at this time.

7. *Make your phone calls at one time.* It's easier to get into the flow if you schedule and conduct your phone calls all at one time. Schedule a break in your work, pick up the phone, and enjoy yourself.

8. *Expect to engage in legitimate conversations when setting appointments.* Starting the sales examination on the phone (establishing chemistry and finding out about some of where it hurts) leads to more effective in-person sales interviews and increases the likelihood that the prospect will keep the appointment.

Don't just call up, say hi, and set the appointment. Expect to engage in a five-to-fifteen minute conversation as you begin the process of selling yourself to the prospective client. Find out about his business, how long he's known the person that referred you into the situation, and start listening for his aches.

9. *Set the appointment for a face-to-face meeting now.* Don't forget to set the appointment for the in-person meeting at the end of the phone call.

A Sample Phone Call

Let's listen in on a typical telephone call between E. J. and Lou, a person he has been referred to:

E. J.: Hi! Is Lou around?
Secretary: Hold on please.
Lou: Lou speaking.
E. J.: Lou? Hi, it's E. J. Jackson. How are you?
Lou: Fine, thanks.
E. J.: Does my name ring a bell?
Lou: Why, yes. Calvin Katt said you would be giving me a call.

If Lou did not recognize E. J.'s name, the following would be said:

E. J.: Does my name ring a bell?
Lou: No, I'm afraid it doesn't. What is this in regard to?
E. J.: Does Calvin Katt's name ring a bell?
Lou: Of course, now I remember. Calvin said you'd be giving me a call.

Back to the conversation:

E. J.: That was nice of Calvin to introduce us. How do you know him?

Lou: Oh, Calvin and I grew up together in Peotone.

E. J.: Did Calvin tell you why he was referring me to you?

Lou: He most certainly did. Calvin said that he just hired you as his new business consultant and that he was so impressed that he thought we should talk, as well.

E. J.: It was nice of him to say that. What do you folks do over there at your company, anyway?

Lou: We make the snake oil that is used in most perfumes and colognes manufactured in this country. Been doing that for about eight hundred years, started in India back in the thirteenth century.

E. J.: Sounds pretty specialized. Do you have much competition in that industry?

Lou: My goodness, yes. A whole flock of fly-by-nighters have come in and try to sell our customers all of the time. We've managed to keep most of our good customers, though.

E. J.: Has the economy affected you any?

Lou: Sure. In times like these, some of the perfume manufacturers try to sneak in synthetics instead of the real thing. It's hurt us some.

E. J.: May I ask why you told Calvin it would be all right for me to call you?

Lou: He seemed so delighted with finally having made a change that I figured there must be a reason why. Today, you need every edge you can get. Calvin said you were going to be helping him in many areas besides just business consulting. All our current consultant does is respond to phone calls—he doesn't even sit down and review our situation on a regular basis. I thought it made sense to talk to you myself.

E. J.: Good. Do you have your calendar available?

Lou: Sure.

E. J.: I'm available for lunch next Tuesday or Friday. What does your schedule look like?

Lou: Friday's much better for me.

E. J.: Eleven forty-five to beat the crowd?

Lou: Perfect.

E. J.: I'll come by at eleven forty-five next Friday and pick you up. I'd like to take a look around your plant after lunch if that would be okay. Please do me a favor: Kindly write down a couple of issues you and I should discuss, perhaps areas of concern that your current consultant isn't addressing. I'd appreciate that.

Lou: Sure. I'll see you next week.

E. J.: Thanks. Bye.

See how easily E. J. involved Lou in a conversation about his business? People love to talk about their businesses and themselves. Notice, too, that E. J. gave Lou some homework to do, a beginning list of his aches to discuss at lunch. This casual chat is typical of good telephone conversations used to set appointments that will result in warm meetings and new clients.

Diagnosis and Rx: Develop a Good Addiction: Use the Telephone Regularly to Screen Patients And Schedule Exams

▸ Although using the telephone to build your practice may be new and uncomfortable now, the more you use the phone effectively to set appointments, keep better contact with your clients and referral sources, and sell work, the more you will fall in love with it.

▸ When utilized properly in the sales process, the telephone offers these powerful benefits:

- Talking on the phone is like a confession, and prospects may say a lot more than they would in person.
- You have the prospect's total attention.
- It's faster than a face-to-face meeting.
- Less can go wrong, because there are fewer variables (such as the way you're dressed and how you act).
- You can separate yourself from the competition more quickly and set a warm note for the face-to-face meeting.

▸ Unfortunately, using the telephone also has these disadvantages:

- You have about eight seconds to capture someone's attention.
- Voice mail and secretaries (also known as gatekeepers) can inhibit contact, unless you know how to get around them and utilize them to your benefit.

▸ Use the phone to:

1. Set appointments with hot leads (like referrals).
2. Maintain and improve contact with clients.
3. Reignite and improve relationshps with referral sources.
4. Set appointments with warm leads.
5. Sell.

▸ The keys to successful telephone selling are as follows:

- Keep your phone calls conversational and casual.
- Use a little ingenuity to reach the prospect.
- Maintain a powerful physiognomy while on the phone.
- Ask yourself, "What would I do if I weren't afraid?"
- Avoid Monday mornings for phone calls.
- Don't worry about interrupting people.
- Make your phone calls at one time.
- Expect to engage in legitimate conversations when setting appointments; start the sales examination on the phone!
- Set the appointment for a face-to-face meeting.

15

The Master "I Hate Selling" (Hey, This Could Be Addictive) System in Action!

In this book, I never said that selling is easy. The purpose of this book is to help you avoid some of the pain and suffering I had to endure in the process of learning how to sell professional services effectively. My goal is to assist you in becoming much more comfortable with and successful at the Greatest Skill in the World. I hope to give you a much different perspective on what selling services really is.

The sales examination approach is designed for you to be in control of the sales process. But that doesn't mean you will find selling a totally painless experience from now on. Failure is an inherent ingredient in the selling process; my goal is to have you endure much less pain and be much more effective than you would have been had you not read this book.

What Did You Learn?

In this book, you learned:

• *What holds professionals back from selling.* Some people never see their excuses and downfalls and thus can't overcome them.

• *The common character traits of the top business producers in the professions—that which separates them from their competition.* Now that you know how and why these people are different, you can model their behavior and the way they are to become much more effective at bringing in business.

• *The distinction between selling and marketing.* Most professionals mistakenly think that marketing must be a formalized process that is best conducted by a marketing department. The essence of marketing is contact—once you decide what you want to sell, you merely have to go to those places where your buyers and referral sources hang out. What do they read? What organizations do they belong to? Who services their industries? Every single contact you have with a client, referral source, and prospective client is marketing. The more contact you have—no matter what the nature of that contact—the more likely they are to buy and keep buying from you.

• *The biggest mistakes in selling.* Now that you know them, you will be much more effective and successful. Some people make the same mistakes over and over because they don't realize what they are doing wrong.

• *The sales examination.* Never again will you have to feel rejected, because now you realize that in order to sell someone, that person must be *qualified.* If he does not qualify as a buyer, he can't be sold. All you can do is conduct the examination to the best of your ability. This knowledge and set of skills are wonderful tools to keep your attitude on an even keel. The examination leads to consistency and more sales success than you've ever dreamed of. Of course, in order for it to work, you do have to apply it!

• *The importance of creating personal chemistry in selling professional services and how to do it.* More so than with selling a tangible product like a copy machine, selling a service requires that the buyer feel comfortable with the service provider. The vast majority of professionals never discover this and thus lose sales they otherwise could have won. Now you have a tremendous edge.

• *How to get people to open up and tell you specifically what their problems, needs, wants, desires, and musts are (where it hurts).* Once you know these concerns, you will find making the sale so much easier. The burden is removed from you; you are in control of the sale. And you learned the importance of commitment in making the sale. Trust me: 99 percent of your competitors haven't recognized and formalized the commitment part of the sales process. Therefore, they think they have buyers but really don't, and so they expend tremendous amounts of wasted energy, time, and money. You can invest your super-valuable time only on those buyers who have told you exactly why they must buy and are committed to doing so.

- *How to thoroughly qualify people for their willingness and ability to pay your fees and the importance of hurts as they relate to getting paid more money.*

- *How to overcome the traps waiting for you in the decision-making process.* More sales are lost here than anyplace else. Now you know how to thoroughly qualify someone for this process, and how specifically to influence it in your favor.

- *The importance of closing on the first call of a sale, and how to write a proposal and/or conduct a presentation (only if necessary) that the prospect wants to buy!*

- *More about closing than 90 percent of your colleagues learn in a lifetime of frustrated selling.* Now you know how to conduct a process where people close themselves.

- *Effective telephone selling.* We discussed selling and conducting yourself to be most effective on the telephone and what a telephone should be used for.

All of this knowledge is the result of fourteen years of interviews, sales calls, and studying the Greatest Skill in the World. You now possess all of the skills necessary to take your closing percentage through the roof.

A Healthy Attitude

It helps to maintain the proper attitude, so I've included those ideas that keep me always at the absolute top of my selling game. Here are some thoughts to remember in order to stay motivated:

1. *Nobody sells everybody.* Lee Iacocca is among the best at selling. How many people don't drive Chryslers? How many people didn't vote for Ronald Reagan or Bill Clinton, two of the world's greatest salespeople? So, next time you find out that you didn't get the business that you thought was in the bag, remember that nobody sells everybody, not even you.

2. *Some sales just aren't meant to be.* Remember the first time you were jilted by a member of the opposite sex? You went through a whole litany of if-only's: "If only I had done this . . ." or "If only I had done that . . . ."

Some relationships aren't in the cards, and we're usually better off without them. Some business relationships aren't meant to be, either. Remember, a very important word in selling is, Next!

3. *They didn't pass the test.* Losing the sale may have had nothing to do with you if you conducted the examination to the best of your ability; in that case, losing the sale simply means the prospect didn't pass the test! Not enough hurt? They didn't pass the test. Weren't committed enough to change? They didn't pass the test. Not willing to pay your fees? They didn't pass the test.

Wouldn't clue you in on the decision-making process? They didn't pass the test. Wouldn't tell you what it would take to sell them? They were playing games and didn't pass the test.

Next!

4. *You have permission to fail.* For the first time in your life, you have permission to fail! In fact, you're supposed to fail when you are out there taking risks. Sometimes, we only learn from our mistakes.

In your role as seller of professional services, failure is acceptable and respectable. Actually, the more failure, the better! The more you fail, the more successes you will have.

5. *Set your goals for no's as well as yes's.* That's right—set goals for the people who won't do business with you! Set goals for people who won't refer business to you or meet you for appointments. The more no's the better, because then you will get more than your share of yes's.

Turn selling into a game that you're good at. If you can learn to feel proud when you've done your best and someone has still told you no, you'll have no problem staying motivated.

6. *Catch a falling star.* Circa 1956 there was a hit song by Perry Como called "Catch a Falling Star." You don't remember it? I still can't figure out why Guns N Roses hasn't done a cover on it yet!

Anyway, to refresh your memory, the song encouraged you to catch and pocket a falling star, and that is what you need to do. You've been putting it off for a long time, so take this opportunity to catch a star and literally put it in your pocket.

Right now—take a stick-it note and write down your salary or income goal for this year and put it in your wallet or on your calendar so that you see it everytime you open it. Place it where you can't avoid it. Do it this very moment.

This is not a new idea, but it took me years to act on it! I don't know why, but having a *written* goal stare you in the face several times a day helps that star come true. I have reached many goals by catching a star and putting it in my pocket. You can and will, too.

7. *There is no perfect sale.* You only have to win by a nose. After reading this book, you have a leg up on 90 percent of the competition, who do nothing more than complain about business, let alone invest in a book on selling.

There isn't a flawless sale. Do most of the examination steps to the best of your ability, and you'll be delighted with the results.

8. *Learn to detach from your patients just like a physician does.* You will meet people who need your help but won't buy your services. Learn to detach from these people. Move on to those you can help and who will allow you to assist.

9. *Keep the proper perspective.* One of my mentors taught me that "selling is merely hysterical activity on the way to the grave." He was right. Put the sales process in the proper perspective.

10. *Be determined to have fun.* What do you enjoy doing? Usually only those activities that you are good at. Be prepared and determined to enjoy sales examining.

11. *Protect your feelings.* Be absolutely committed to not having your feelings hurt by anyone. You're an adult; it's time to get control over the way you react to situations.

There is a distinction between what happens to us (the facts) and our interpretation of the situation. When someone doesn't return your phone call, the *fact* is that they didn't return your phone call!

Often, we infer that this action (or lack thereof) means they weren't interested, they are jerking us around, we've lost the sale, and so on. As soon as you stop playing these types of mind games with yourself, the happier you will be at building your practice.

12. *Remember: You're already successful!* The best definition of success I've ever seen is attributed to a man who many would consider to be the world's greatest motivational speaker, the late Earl Nightingale. It took him thirty years of study and thought to come up with this: "Success is the progressive realization of a worthy goal."

Success is not the Lexus coupe you've always wanted—that's a goal! Don't confuse the two. You are successful because you've read this book; you've done something to improve yourself on your way to bringing in more business.

13. *You don't need the business!* Some of the most valuable coaching I've ever received, which I now pass along to you, is that you are not going to starve to death tomorrow morning and you don't *need* the business.

I'm not suggesting you be arrogant. But this attitude is extremely powerful because it puts you in the driver's seat. Do you want the business? Perhaps. When you stop *needing* the business, people won't beat you up over fees anymore. Prospective buyers are attracted to service providers who are already very successful and don't need the business.

14. *What would you do if you weren't afraid?* Often, participants in a seminar will ask me a question like: "Allan, do you really say that to a client?" or "Do you really do that?" Of course I say and do these things—there is no theory in this book, only that which I've practiced and learned from the top business producers in the professions.

As I get older, and the concept of mortality becomes clearer, I've become committed to the fact that I don't want to go to my grave asking the following question of myself: "Hey Allan, what would you have done differently in your life, had you not been afraid to do it?" By then it's too late!

And that's the way I handle my selling—I ask the questions that need to be asked, although I might be afraid. I make the calls that should be made. I ask things of people that I might not otherwise ask, had I been afraid.

The single best remover of fear in every situation has been to ask myself the following question: "What would you do if you weren't afraid?"

For some unknown reason, asking yourself this simple question has the miraculous ability to remove your fear. Freed of your fear, you can now pick up the phone, ask the question, make the request, and do what needs to be done to make more sales and take more risks.

Let's end the book with "I'd Pick More Daisies" (anonymous):

> If I had my life to live over, I'd pick more daisies. I'd try to make more mistakes next time. I would be sillier than I had been this trip. I would relax, I would limber up. I know very few things I would take seriously. I would take more trips, travel lighter. I would be crazier. I would be less hygienic. I would take more chances. I would climb more mountains, swim more rivers, and watch more sunsets. I would eat more ice cream and less beans. I would have more actual troubles and fewer imagined ones.
>
> You see, I am one of those people who live practically and sensibly and sanely, hour after hour, day after day . . . Oh, I have my mad moments and if I had it to do over

again, I'd have more of them; in fact, I'd try to have nothing else. Just moments, one after another, instead of living so many minutes ahead. I have been one of these people who never go anywhere without a thermometer, a hot water bottle, a gargle, a raincoat, and a road map.

If I had to live my life over, I would start barefooted earlier in the spring and stay that way later in the fall. I'd play hookey more, I would ride more merry-go-rounds and swing more. I would do more water and sun fun things. I'd turn more somersaults and roll in the grass and go barefoot all over.

If I had my life to live over, I'd spend more time at fun places. I'd try to be more in touch with God and those I love. I'd pray aloud more and not care what people think of me. I'd give more of me and take more of you. I'd just be me more and more . . .

. . . Yes, I'd pick more daisies next time.

Good selling!

Index